# Decentralized Decision-Making in Schools

# Decentralized Decision-Making in Schools

*The Theory and Evidence on School-Based Management*

Felipe Barrera-Osorio
Tazeen Fasih
and
Harry Anthony Patrinos
with Lucrecia Santibáñez

**THE WORLD BANK**
**Washington, D.C.**

© 2009 The International Bank for Reconstruction and Development / The World Bank
1818 H Street NW
Washington DC 20433
Telephone: 202-473-1000
Internet: www.worldbank.org
E-mail: feedback@worldbank.org

1 2 3 4 12 11 10 09

This volume is a product of the staff of the International Bank for Reconstruction and Development / The World Bank. The findings, interpretations, and conclusions expressed in this volume do not necessarily reflect the views of the Executive Directors of The World Bank or the governments they represent.

The World Bank does not guarantee the accuracy of the data included in this work. The boundaries, colors, denominations, and other information shown on any map in this work do not imply any judgment on the part of The World Bank concerning the legal status of any territory or the endorsement or acceptance of such boundaries.

ISBN: 978-0-8213-7969-1
eISBN: 978-0-8213-7970-7
DOI: 10.1596/978-0-8213-7969-1

Library of Congress Cataloging-in-Publication Data

Barrera-Osorio, Felipe.
 Directions in development : decentralized decision-making in schools the theory and evidence on school-based management / Felipe Barrera-Osorio, Tazeen Fasih, and Harry Anthony Patrinos; with Lucrecia Santibáñez.
  p. cm.
 Includes bibliographical references and index.
 ISBN 978-0-8213-7969-1 (alk. paper) — ISBN 978-0-8213-7970-7 (electronic)
 1. Schools—Decentralization. 2. School management and organization. 3. Decision making.
I. Barrera-Osorio, Felipe. II. Fasih, Tazeen, 1972- III. Title.
LB2862P38 2009
379.1'535—dc22

                                                                                    2009010776

Cover photo by Julio Pantoja/World Bank Photo Library. Students and teacher in the town school, Santa Terezinha, in Vila Da Canoas, in the Amazon region of Brazil, near Manaus.
Cover design: Naylor Design, Inc.

# Contents

## Boxes

## Figures

## Tables

# Foreword

In both the developed and developing worlds, government attempts to improve education have been mostly about providing more classrooms, more teachers, and more textbooks to schools. There is growing evidence, however, that more inputs are not enough to make schools work better. One important reason why education systems are failing to provide children with a solid education is the weak accountability relationships among policy makers, education providers, and the citizens and students whom they serve. It is not surprising then that the transfer of some decision-making power to schools has become a popular reform over the past decade.

School-based management (SBM) puts power in the hands of the frontline providers and parents to improve their schools. Its basic premise is that people who have the most to gain or lose—students and their parents—and those who know what actually goes on in the classroom and school—teachers and school principals—should have both greater authority and greater accountability than they do now with respect to school performance.

However, while there is evidence that SBM can improve the quality of teaching and learning in schools, our evidence base is limited. *Decentralized Decision-Making in Schools* adds to that knowledge base by distilling the lessons from countries with different SBM arrangements, reviews the findings from analytical studies, and presents the policy choices that emerge from those lessons and findings.

During the past two decades, educational differences between richer and poorer countries, as measured by enrollment rates and average years of schooling, have narrowed—but the global gap in student achievement levels remains very wide. Where successful, SBM offers the potential to close that learning gap.

Elizabeth M. King
Director, Education
Human Development Network
The World Bank

# Preface

School-based management has become a very popular movement over the last decade. The World Bank's work on school-based management emerged from a need to better define the concept, review the evidence, support impact assessments in various countries, and provide feedback to project teams. The authors took detailed stock of the existing literature on school-based management and then identified several cases that the Bank was supporting in various countries. The authors present as well general guidance on how to evaluate school-based management programs. The Bank continues to support and oversee a number of impact evaluations of school-based management programs in an array of countries.

## About This Book

The eighth meeting of the High-Level Group on Education for All (EFA-HLG) was held in Oslo, Norway, December 16–18, 2008. It provided world leaders with an opportunity to reassert the importance of education and the need to achieve the EFA goals. The EFA-HLG serves as the focal point for the political commitment, as well as the technical and financial resource mobilization, needed to achieve the six EFA goals:

1. Expand early childhood care and education
2. Provide free and compulsory primary education for all
3. Promote learning and life skills for young people and adults
4. Increase adult literacy by 50 percent
5. Achieve gender parity by 2005, gender equality by 2015
6. Improve the quality of education.

The 2008 meeting was pivotal for the EFA movement. It signified the midpoint between the year 2000, when developing and donor countries alike reinforced their commitments to the six goals, and the year 2015, the target year for achieving those goals. Similarly, it was the midpoint between the declaration and projected achievement of the Millennium Development Goal of universal primary school completion. Most important, 2008 was the last chance for children to begin first grade in order to complete sixth grade by 2015.

This book, *Decentralized Decision-Making in Schools: The Theory and Evidence on School-Based Management*, was produced for the December 2008 meeting by a team led by Robin Horn, education sector manager of the Human Development Department of the World Bank. The work received the generous support of the Norwegian government. The Kingdom of Norway has provided grant funding to the World Bank to scale up analyses in three areas critical to achieving EFA goals: education in fragile states, financing of education in developing countries, and management and accountability in education.

# Acknowledgments

We are indebted to many people who helped us in the preparation of this book. For their valuable contributions, suggestions, and feedback, we would like to thank Martha Ainsworth, Shaista Baksh, Regina Bendokat, Raja Bentaouet-Kattan, Luis Benveniste, Erik Bloom, Bong Gun Chung, Amit Dar, Carmen Ana Deseda, Shantayanan Devarajan, Emanuela di Gropello, Ariel Fiszbein, Vicente A. Garcia-Moreno, Paul Gertler, Verónica Grigera, April Harding, Robin Horn, Dingyong Hou, Emmanuel Jimenez, Ruth Kagia, Elizabeth King, Nandini Krishnan, Heather Layton, Maureen Lewis, Muna Salih Meky, Benoit Millot, Michael Mills, Mamta Murthi, Michelle Riboud, Halsey Rogers, Marta Rubio-Codina, Anna Maria Sant'Anna, Leopold Sarr, Kouassi Soman, Jee-Peng Tan, Emiliana Vegas, Raisa Venalainen, Christel Vermeersch, and Inosha Wickramasekera. During the authors' workshop in March 2007, excellent seminars were delivered by Lorenzo-Gomez Morin (formerly undersecretary of basic education, Mexico) and Thomas Cook (Northwestern University). Fiona MacKintosh provided excellent editing of the content, and Victoriano Arias formatted the document. Grant funding from the Norwegian government is gratefully acknowledged.

# Abbreviations

| | |
|---|---|
| ACEs | Associations for Community Education (Asociacíon Comunitana de Educación) [El Salvador] |
| AGEs | Support to School Management Program (Apoyo a la Gestión Escolar) [Mexico] |
| BOS | School Operational Assistance (Bantuan Operasional Sekolah) [Indonesia] |
| COGES | school management committees (Comité de Gestion de l'Etablissement Scolaire) [Niger] |
| DD | difference-in-differences |
| EDUCO | Education with Community Participation (Educación con Participación de la Comunidad) [El Salvador] |
| EQIP | Education Quality Improvement Project [Cambodia] |
| ETP | Extra Teacher Program [Kenya] |
| FAF | Association of Teachers [Madagascar] |
| FRAM | Association of Parents of School Children [Madagascar] |
| GDP | gross domestic product |
| ICS | International Child Support Africa |
| IV | instrumental variable |

| | |
|---|---|
| ME | matching estimation |
| NGO | nongovernmental organization |
| OECD | Organisation for Economic Co-operation and Development |
| PDE | Plan for the Development of the School (Plano de Desenvolvimiento da Escola) [Brazil] |
| PEC | Quality Schools Program (Programa Escuelas de Calidad) [Mexico] |
| PROHECO | Community-Based Education Program (Proyecto Hondureño de Educación Comunitaria) [Honduras] |
| PRONADE | Community-Managed Program for Educational Development (Programa Nacional de Autogestión para el Desarrollo Educativo) [Guatemala] |
| PTA | parent-teacher association |
| RDD | regression discontinuity design |
| SBM | school-based management |
| SDP | Comer School Development Program |
| SMC | school management committee |
| SMI | School Management Initiative [Hong Kong, China] |
| WDR | *World Development Report* |
| WSD | whole school development |

*All dollar amounts are U.S. dollars, unless otherwise indicated.*

# Overview

*For more than 100 years the lack of a school management methodology has been the cause of countless complaints. But it has been only in the last 30 years that efforts have been made to find a solution to this problem. And, what has resulted so far? Schools continue exactly the same as before.*

– Jan Amos Comenius, 1632

Despite the clear commitment of governments and international agencies to the education sector, efficient and equitable access remains elusive for many populations—especially for girls, indigenous peoples, and other poor and marginalized groups. Many international initiatives focus on these access issues with great commitment, but even where the vast majority of children do have access to education facilities, the quality of that education often is very poor. This fact increasingly is apparent in the scores from international learning assessments on which most students from developing countries do not excel. Evidence has shown that merely increasing resource allocation without also introducing institutional reforms in the education sector will not increase equity or improve the quality of education.

Governments around the world are introducing a range of strategies aimed at improving the financing and delivery of education services, and recently they have added an emphasis on improving quality as well as increasing quantity (in terms of enrollment rates). The decentralization of educational decision making is one such strategy. Advocates of this strategy maintain that decentralizing decision making encourages demand for a higher quality of education and ensures that schools reflect local priorities and values. By giving a voice and decision-making power to local stakeholders who know more about the local education systems than do central policy makers, decentralization can improve educational outcomes and increase client satisfaction. One way to decentralize decision-making power in education is known popularly as school-based management (SBM). There are other names for this concept, but they all refer to the decentralization of authority from the central government to the school level. SBM emphasizes the individual school (represented by any combination of principals, teachers, parents, students, and other members of the school community) as the main decision-making authority, and holds that this shift in the formulating of decisions would lead to improvement in the delivery of education.

## What Is School-Based Management?

School-based management is the decentralization of authority from the central government to the school level (Caldwell 2005). In the words of Malen, Ogawa, and Kranz (1990), "School-based management can be viewed conceptually as a formal alteration of governance structures, as a form of decentralization that identifies the individual school as the primary unit of improvement and relies on the redistribution of decision-making authority as the primary means through which improvement might be stimulated and sustained" (p. 290).

There have been many SBM reforms in developing countries. A review of the World Bank education portfolio for fiscal years 2000–06 reveals that about 10 percent of all projects support SBM, a total of 15 among approximately 157 projects. These projects represent $1.7 billion[1]— 23 percent of the Bank's lending for basic education or 18 percent of its total education financing (see table 1).

The majority of the SBM projects in the current portfolio are in Latin American and South Asian countries, including Argentina, Bangladesh, Guatemala, Honduras, India, Mexico, and Sri Lanka. There also are two Bank-supported SBM projects in Europe and Central Asia (in the former Yugoslav Republic of Macedonia and in Serbia and Montenegro), and one each in East Asia and the Pacific (the Philippines), the Middle East and North Africa (Lebanon), and sub-Saharan Africa (Lesotho). Other

**Table 1    School-Based Management in World Bank–Financed Education Projects**

|  | Total | SBM | Percent of total |
|---|---|---|---|
| Education projects (number) | 157 | 15 | 10 |
| Education lending ($ millions) | 9.49 | 1.70 | 18 |
| Basic education lending ($ millions) | 7.44 | 1.70 | 23 |

*Source:* World Bank's List of Education Projects, FY00–06.
*Note:* SBM = school-based management. "Lending" indicates the total amount committed by the International Bank for Reconstruction and Development/International Development Association (IDA).

projects and programs have been introduced more recently in The Gambia, Madagascar, and Senegal. All of these reforms are reviewed in chapter 2.

Most SBM projects involve some sort of transfer of responsibility and decision making—usually the responsibility for school operations—to a combination of principals, teachers, parents, and other school community members. These projects try to empower principals and teachers and strengthen their professional motivation, thereby enhancing their sense of ownership of the school. They also seek to involve the local community in a meaningful way, making decisions about their local school. By these means, the projects aim to increase the speed and relevance of school-level decision making.

Most SBM projects work through some sort of school committee (or school council or school management committee). The school committee may (1) monitor the school's performance, for example, in test scores or teacher and student attendance; (2) raise funds and create endowments for the school; (3) appoint, suspend, dismiss, and remove teachers, and ensure that teachers' salaries are paid regularly[2]; and (4) albeit rarely, approve annual budgets, including the development budget, and examine monthly financial statements.

Several of these projects seek to strengthen parents' involvement in the management of the school by getting them involved in the school committee or council. Parents participate voluntarily and take on various responsibilities, ranging from the assessment of student learning to financial management. In some projects, parents are involved directly in the school's management by being custodians of the funds received and verifying the purchases and contracts made by the school. School councils also may be required to develop some sort of school improvement plan.

## Different Forms of School-Based Management

SBM programs take many different forms in terms of who has the power to make decisions and how much decision-making authority devolves to the school level. Whereas some programs transfer authority only to school principals or teachers, others encourage or mandate parental and community participation, often through their active membership in school committees. In general, SBM programs devolve authority over one or more activities. These can be any of the following: (1) budget allocations, (2) hiring and firing of teachers and other school staff, (3) curriculum development, (4) procurement of textbooks and other educational materials, (5) infrastructure improvement, and (6) monitoring and evaluation of teacher performance and student learning outcomes. Although we define SBM broadly to include community-based management and parental participation mechanisms, in this review, explicitly, we do not include stand-alone, or one-off, school grants programs that are not meant to be permanent alterations in school management.

SBM reforms are far from uniform and they encompass a wide variety of strategies. Each program is shaped by the objectives of the reformers and by the broader national policy and social context in which it is created. There are two key dimensions to the devolution of decision making—the degree of autonomy being devolved (what) and the people to whom the decision-making authority is devolved (who). With so many possible combinations of these two dimensions, almost every SBM reform is unique. It is estimated that there are more than 800 SBM models in the United States alone, and globally SBM reforms vary even more widely (Rowan, Camburn, and Barnes 2004).

SBM programs lie along a continuum in the degree to which decision making is devolved to the school. "Weak" SBM reforms at one end of the continuum can be described as those in which schools have limited autonomy, usually over issues concerning instructional methods or planning for school improvement (for example, Mexico's Quality Schools Program [Programa Escuelas de Calidad; PEC]). A weak version of SBM might be characterized by school councils that play only an advisory role (as happens, for example, in schools in Edmonton [Canada], Senegal, and Thailand). A "strong" form of SBM is characterized by school councils that receive funds directly from the central or other relevant level of government and have been granted the responsibility for hiring and firing teachers and principals and/or for setting curricula (as in the EDUCO program in El Salvador). Strong forms of SBM include education systems in which parents have complete choice and control over public education and where all decisions concerning the operational, financial, and educational management of schools are in the hands of school councils or school administrators (as, for example, in the Netherlands or the charter school reforms in Qatar). It is interesting to note that at the strong end of the continuum, the distinction between public and private schools becomes blurred.

The other key dimension of SBM is who is given responsibility for the devolved functions. There are four models that typify the various arrangements included in SBM reforms:

1. *administrative-control SBM*—in which the authority is devolved to the school principal
2. *professional-control SBM*—in which teachers hold the main decision-making authority so as to use their knowledge of the school and its students
3. *community-control SBM*—in which parents have the major decision-making authority
4. *balanced-control SBM*—in which decision-making authority is shared by parents and teachers.

In practice, an SBM program usually adopts a blend of the four models. In most cases, a formal legal entity (a school council or school management committee) consists of the principal, teachers, and, in almost all cases, community representatives. The Support to School Management Program (Apoyo a la Gestión Escolar; AGEs) in rural Mexico gives minimal autonomy to school councils, which are led mainly by parents. New Zealand's model is highly autonomous, however, with most decision-making power lying with the parents. Another extreme is the case of the Netherlands, where since 1985 the government has given school principals authority over a large number of functions with the goal of increasing efficiency, and has allowed parents to create new schools that meet their own specific cultural and religious needs. In Qatar, the Supreme Education Council implemented a school reform that effectively introduced the charter school model into the country and allowed any parental group, teacher, or other organization to open up a publicly funded, privately run school.

However, by making individual schools the focus of educational policy change, SBM does not assume that governments will be completely out of the decision-making picture. Public schools always will exist in some larger policy and administrative context that affects their operations. The key is to identify precisely what the government's role in decision making should be, given each political and social context.

## School-Based Management Reforms around the World

School-based management is very popular. SBM-type reforms have been introduced in countries with diverse educational systems, such as Australia,

Canada, Israel, and the United States—some going back 30 years. There are many reasons for this popularity. SBM has the potential to be a low-cost means of making public spending on education more efficient by increasing the accountability of the agents involved and by empowering the clients to improve learning outcomes. And by putting power in the hands of the service end users (people who are doing the educating or have children being educated), SBM eventually produces better school management that is more cognizant of and responsive to the needs of those end users, thus creating a better and more conducive learning environment for the students.

The potential benefits of such a system are large and involve only marginal costs. These benefits can include

- more input and resources from parents (whether in cash or in-kind)
- more effective use of resources because those making the decisions for each school are intimately acquainted with its needs
- a higher quality of education as a result of more efficient and transparent use of resources
- a more open and welcoming school environment because the community is involved in its management
- increased participation of all local stakeholders in the decision-making processes, leading to more collegial relationships and increased satisfaction
- improved student performance as a result of reduced repetition rates, reduced dropout rates, and (eventually) better learning outcomes.

Across the countries in the Organisation for Economic Co-operation and Development (OECD) there is a trend toward increasing autonomy, devolving responsibility, and encouraging responsiveness to local needs, all with the objective of raising performance levels (OECD 2004). Most countries whose students perform well in international student achievement tests give their local authorities and schools substantial autonomy over adapting and implementing educational content, allocating and managing resources, or both. With a few exceptions, most students in OECD countries are enrolled in schools in which teachers and stakeholders play a role in deciding what courses are offered and how money is spent within the school. There is a strong positive relationship between school autonomy and student performance. Moreover, greater school autonomy is not necessarily associated with wider disparities in school performance among schools, as long as governments provide a framework in which more poorly performing schools receive needed support to help them improve. In fact, Finland and Sweden (which are among those countries with the highest degree of school autonomy on many Programme for International Student Assessment measures) and Iceland have the smallest performance differences among schools (OECD 2004).

This study reviews more than 20 country experiences with SBM in Latin America and the Caribbean, Africa, Asia, and the Middle East and North Africa, as well as in more developed countries, such as Australia, the Netherlands, New Zealand, the United Kingdom, and the United States. For each of these countries, we include a brief description of the SBM reform along with any evidence regarding its impact on a variety of indicators, ranging from student test scores and dropout and repetition rates to parent and teacher perceptions of the reform's benefits. Here we start by giving a brief description of the SBM programs implemented in various countries, arranged by region.

### Latin America and the Caribbean
In El Salvador, the SBM reform was implemented in 1991 under the name EDUCO (Education with Community Participation; [Educación con Participación de la Comunidad]). EDUCO schools are publicly funded, and their students receive (in addition to free tuition and textbooks) free uniforms, registration, and basic school supplies. In return, parents are expected to contribute meals, time, and, in some cases, their labor to improve schools (Edge 2000). The distinguishing feature of EDUCO schools is the Community Education Association (Asociación Comunitaria de Educación; [ACE]). Each EDUCO school has one ACE with five community-elected members. ACEs receive funds directly from the Ministry of Education and are responsible for enacting and implementing ministry and community policies; and for hiring, firing, and monitoring teachers (Sawada and Ragatz 2005). Similar projects have been implemented in Honduras (Community-Based Education Program [Proyecto Hondureño de Educación Comunitaria; {PROHECO}]), Guatemala (Community-Managed Program for Educational Development [Programa Nacional de Autogestión para el Desarrollo Educativo; {PRONADE}]), and Nicaragua.

In 2001, Mexico implemented PEC. This program is intended to provide more autonomy to schools by giving them annual grants of up to $5,000 to improve educational quality (Skoufias and Shapiro 2006). In exchange for PEC grants, schools must prepare an educational improvement plan that outlines how they will use the grant. Parent associations must be involved in the design, implementation, and monitoring of the plan. In the first 4 years, about 80 percent of the grant must be spent on school materials and facilities. In the fifth year, only part of the money must be spent on such goods, with a large proportion of the grant going to fund teacher training and development. Participation in PEC is voluntary, but the program targets disadvantaged urban schools. A similar reform was undertaken in Brazil with the Community-Based Education Program (Plano de Desenvolvimiento da Escola; PDE), a program designed to make schools more responsive to students and their communities. Under the PDE, schools engage in a self-evaluation, develop a school plan focusing on two or three "efficiency factors" (one of which has to be effective teaching and learning), and design actions intended to address those factors. In turn, the Fund for the Strengthening of Schools (Fundescola), a program created by Brazil's Ministry of Education, provides funds to support PDE schools' goals and projects (Carnoy et al. 2008).

Another SBM reform undertaken in Mexico was AGEs. This program, begun in 1996, provides cash grants ($500–$700, depending on the school's size) and training to parent associations. The money may be spent on any educational activity that an association deems to be appropriate. In most instances, spending is limited to improvements to school facilities.

### Africa

Various SBM reforms are under way in Africa. Some of the earlier efforts were conceived under the umbrella of "whole school development" (WSD), a package of reforms aimed at improving school management, in-service training, and monitoring and evaluation, among other things (Akyeampong 2004). This holistic approach to school improvement has been implemented, with some variations, in such countries as Ghana and South Africa.

In Kenya, community members participate in schools by serving on school committees. These committees or parent-teacher associations (PTAs) consist of elected parents and representatives from the District Education Board. In general, a committee's authority is limited to suggesting promotions and transfers of teachers to the Ministry of Education, overseeing expenditures from capitation grants, and participating in the design and implementation of school development plans. A recent pilot program in Kenya—the Extra Teacher Program (ETP)—provided funds to 140 schools randomly selected from a pool of 210 schools to hire an extra teacher for first-grade classes. The program was funded by the World Bank and International Child Support Africa (ICS), a nongovernmental organization (NGO) working with schools in the region. Among the 140 schools sampled to receive funding to hire a contract teacher from the local area, 70 schools were selected randomly to participate in an SBM intervention in which school committees monitored the performance of these contract teachers. In each SBM school, the school committee held a formal review meeting at the end of the program's first school year (2005) to assess the contract teacher's performance and decide whether to renew his or her contract or to make a replacement. To prepare the school committees for this task, the ICS gave committee members a short, focused training course on how to monitor the contract teacher's performance, including techniques for soliciting input from parents and checking teacher attendance. A subcommittee of first-graders' parents was formed to evaluate the contract teacher and to deliver a performance report at the end of the first year (Duflo, Dupas, and Kremer 2007).

In several African countries, introducing free primary education meant abolishing school fees that previously had been paid by parents. The expenditures that used to be covered by these fees are now funded by grants (sometimes called capitation grants) from the central government. For example, in countries like The Gambia, Ghana, Madagascar, Niger, Rwanda, and Senegal, the government gives a direct grant to schools, the amount of which is calculated on a per-student basis. School councils may use these capitation grants to purchase school supplies, fund teacher training, and improve facilities. In some cases (as in Ghana and Rwanda), the grants may be used to give teachers bonus allowances (dependent on the successful completion of requirements set between teacher and principal) and/or to support the full cost (salary and bonus) of teachers hired on a fixed-term contract (in Ghana, Niger, Rwanda, and in some forms of SBM in Madagascar).

## Asia

In 1991, Hong Kong, China, began implementing a series of SBM reforms mirroring those in Australia, the United Kingdom, and the United States (Dimmock and Walker 1998b; Wong 2003). In 1997, the Hong Kong, China, Education Commission approved the School Management Initiative (SMI), which broadened the scope of the original reform and gave school management committees autonomy over decisions regarding personnel, financial matters, and curriculum design and delivery (Wong 2003). Schools may opt into the SMI voluntarily.

In Cambodia, the SBM program is called the Education Quality Improvement Project (EQIP) School Grants Program. It began in Takeo Province in 1998 with a pilot group of 10 clusters, and expanded to include roughly 1,000 schools in three provinces between 1998 and 2003. EQIP schools receive cash grants that are invested in items on a priority list drawn up collectively by the participating schools.

In Indonesia, the School Operational Assistance (Bantuan Operasional Sekolah; BOS) program has introduced a limited form of SBM. Under the program, school committees were set up in 2005 to run SBM programs. All schools in Indonesia receive block grants based on a per-student formula, but school committees have control only over nonsalary operational expenditures.

### Middle East and North Africa

In an effort to improve educational quality in Israel, the municipality of Jerusalem gradually introduced SBM into 60 of the city's 74 schools over a period of 4 years, beginning in 1997. As part of the SBM reform, schools are expected to develop well-defined goals and a clear work plan and to carry out extensive monitoring and assessment of educational outcomes. In return, schools may manage part of their budgets (the part that is not controlled by the central government) and have some authority over personnel matters and the establishment of a school council (Nir 2002).

In 2001, the government of Qatar hired the RAND Corporation to design a reform of its education system. Beginning in 2003, a new system of independent schools was put in place. These independent schools (similar to charter schools in the United States) receive government funding but are managed by the schools themselves. The goals of the new system are first to improve education in Qatar by creating a variety of alternative kinds of schools with different missions, curricula, pedagogy, and resource allocation models; and then to hold all schools accountable for the quality of the education they provide. A contracting mechanism is used to select the operators of new or existing schools so that many different stakeholders become actively engaged in the school system. Operators may be groups of educators or parents, private education management organizations or schools, or any other entity capable of providing educational and financial guarantees of its ability to attract a sufficient number of students and educate them successfully. The rules under which independent schools operate are referred to as "contract guidelines" and are similar to those in any contract that lays out each party's obligations. Students who were eligible for government funding under the old system continue to be eligible under the new independent school system, and the government pays the costs of their schooling directly to their schools' operators.

### Other Countries

SBM also has been in operation in Australia, Canada, and New Zealand for more than 25 years. Throughout the 1980s and 1990s, the British government increasingly devolved authority and autonomy to parents and teachers. The most important reform during that time was the 1988 Education Reform Act, which created two categories of schools—locally managed and grant-maintained schools. In both of these models, school governing bodies are given authority and autonomy over a school's budget and its day-to-day operations. Both categories of schools also have the power to hire and fire all teaching and nonteaching staff. Unfortunately, there are no rigorous evaluations of the Australian, New Zealand, or UK programs so there is no convincing evidence of the effects of these reforms on student achievement. The United States also has implemented various forms of SBM over the last 30 years, including programs in Florida, Chicago (Illinois), New York, and Virginia.

## Can School-Based Management Work?

When the who and the what of SBM have been defined, it is hoped that all the actors and stakeholders at the school level will work together in a collegial way to put school-based authority and accountability into practice. However, as we will see in chapter 2, there is little evidence to show that this is actually what happens.

There are a few well-documented cases of SBM and some documented cases of success, but the sample of carefully documented, rigorous SBM impact evaluations since 1995 is considerably smaller than the number of known SBM programs around the world. This situation is improving, and various rigorous evaluations and randomized experiments of SBM are being carried out in different countries—but currently we know little. Moreover, some of the few rigorous studies that we review here have problems. In most cases, for example, the lack of randomized experiments has forced researchers to carry out retrospective analyses. Also, depending on the quantity of data available, most researchers have had to search for instrumental variables to identify the intervention, as well as other econometric techniques. That raises questions about the validity of the chosen instruments. Those studies that used over-time differences between beneficiary and nonbeneficiary groups or tried to match beneficiaries with a similar nonbeneficiary group were limited by a lack of data, either because the baseline data were not rich enough or because there was no preprogram trend information. These shortcomings have undermined the conclusions of the literature produced so far on the impact of SBM.

Nevertheless, these studies represent an important attempt to quantify the impact of some SBM programs on educational outcomes. It may be argued that the studies reviewed here reduce the bias undoubtedly present in simple comparisons and, in this way, they produce important advances in our understanding of the impact of SBM policies. Despite the fact that it is very difficult to quantify the effects of the outcome variables of interest because of differences in metrics across studies, it is possible to reach some conclusions about the impact of SBM on the basis of the more rigorous analyses:

- Some studies found that SBM policies actually changed the dynamics of the school, either because parents got more involved or because teachers' actions changed.
- Several studies presented evidence that SBM had an reducing impact on repetition rates; failure rates; and, to a lesser degree, dropout rates.
- The studies that had access to standardized test scores yielded mixed evidence. One of the studies that yielded strong positive evidence supported by a rigorous evaluation strategy was done in Kenya, where an SBM initiative implemented in randomly selected schools had significant positive effects on student test scores. These positive outcomes were the result of a combination of reduced class sizes, more teacher incentives, and greater parental oversight (Duflo, Dupas, and Kremer 2007).

The general finding that SBM has had a positive impact on some variables—mainly in reducing repetition and failure and in improving attendance rates (in contrast to its mixed results on test scores) could be the result of timing. It is a reasonable rule of thumb that SBM needs approximately 5 years to bring about fundamental changes at the school level and about 8 years to produce changes in difficult-to-modify indicators, such as test scores. This has been the experience in the United States, where at least 29 of the 800 SBM experiments have been evaluated at least once. Moreover, it is possible to argue that school learning is a cumulative process and that students need to have been exposed to SBM for at least 5 years to enjoy the potential benefits of the reform.

## Evaluating School-Based Management Initiatives

In general terms, a good evaluation should include the following three important steps (Gertler, Patrinos, and Rubio-Codina 2007):

1. *Clearly define the intervention*—All interventions modify margins and incentives differently for different stakeholders. It is critical to define what is being modified in the program, the new set of incentives, and to whom the modifications apply.
2. *Describe how the intervention is expected to achieve the final desired outcomes*—Understanding how the intervention will lead to the desired result is fundamental for the evaluation. In general terms, sound economic theory should guide the analysis of how the intervention will affect the desired outcomes.
3. *Define the identification strategy*—An identification strategy is the mechanism by which causal effects may be attributed between an intervention (for example, the SBM program) and a set of outcome variables (such as dropout rates or standardized test scores). To attribute to the program any changes in outcome variables, it is necessary to overcome the problems of self-selection.

Those three steps, which are essential to performing a rigorous impact evaluation, are particularly challenging in the case of SBM programs. Defining the intervention is very difficult because of the complexity of the SBM concept. How the intervention is likely to achieve the desired results will depend on the complexity of the specific intervention. Finally, identifying causal effects is difficult because of the three sources of bias—self-selection of schools, selection of schools by authorities, and the process by which students are enrolled in the SBM schools.

Based on our review of SBM impact studies, we believe that performing retrospective evaluations (or ones based on programs already being implemented and having limited data) is extremely difficult. It is preferable to carry out prospective evaluations on programs that have yet to be implemented so that baseline (preintervention) data may be collected in advance.

Ideally, any study trying to assess the effects of SBM would use some form of randomization. Only one of the country cases we reviewed (Kenya) had evaluated an SBM strategy using explicit randomizing of treatment and control schools. However, if randomizing is not an option, two other strategies may be used instead. First, when the program is targeted using some continuous variable as the entry criterion, it may be helpful to use a regression discontinuity design (RDD) procedure. With RDD, the estimation will yield the true effect of the intervention without the need for randomizing. RDD is a more flexible procedure than propensity matching estimation, for instance, especially when it is used to evaluate programs that already are operating. The second useful strategy is a nonrandom phase-in strategy. For this evaluation method to be technically sound, it is critical to show that the second group to be studied is the right counterfactual for the group that initially entered the program— that is, the groups need to have similar pretreatment observable characteristics. To use this procedure, it is essential to have good preintervention data on both groups. Good postintervention data also are needed to carry out the analyses.

In sum, the design and initial setup of SBM projects are extremely important, perhaps more so than in any other education intervention. Beyond that finding, all we can conclude is that different types of SBM reforms work under different circumstances.

## Notes

1. A billion is 1,000 millions.
2. This is usually seen only under the most radical interpretations of SBM, primarily in postconflict or post–natural disaster countries. Examples in the current World Bank portfolio include EDUCO in El Salvador, or PRONADE and PROHECO in Guatemala and Honduras, respectively; additional examples are in other countries such as Qatar or some SBM versions in Madagascar.

# CHAPTER 1

# What Is School-Based Management?

School-based management reforms have become increasingly popular in many countries. However, not all SBM reforms are created equal. In fact, there are many different types and flavors of SBM reforms around the world. This chapter describes the theory behind SBM. It presents a typology for SBM and constructs a conceptual framework for the analysis of such reforms, including the mechanisms through which SBM is thought to improve outcomes (such as student achievement or parental participation).

## School-Based Management Defined

SBM is the decentralization of authority from the central government to the school level (Caldwell 2005). In the words of Malen, Ogawa, and Kranz (1990), "School-based management can be viewed conceptually as a formal alteration of governance structures, as a form of decentralization that identifies the individual school as the primary unit of improvement and relies on the redistribution of decision-making authority as the primary means through which improvement might be stimulated and sustained" (p. 290).

Thus, in SBM, responsibility for and decision-making authority over school operations are transferred to principals, teachers, parents, and sometimes to students and other school community members. However, these school-level actors have to conform to or operate within a set of policies determined by the central government. SBM programs exist in many different forms, both in terms of who has the power to make decisions and in terms of the degree of decision making devolved to the school level. Whereas some programs transfer authority only to principals or teachers, others encourage or mandate parental and community participation, often as members of school committees (or school councils, school management committees). In general, SBM programs transfer authority over one or more of the following activities: budget (allocating budget), personnel management (hiring and firing teachers and other school staff), pedagogy (developing curriculum), maintenance and infrastructure (procuring textbooks and other educational materials, improving infrastructure), and monitoring and evaluation (monitoring and evaluating teacher performance and student learning outcomes) (see table 1.1).

## The Theory behind School-Based Management

Good education involves not only physical input—such as classrooms, teachers, and textbooks—but also incentives that lead to better instruction and learning. Education systems place extreme demands on the managerial, technical, and financial capacity of governments; thus, education as a service is too complex to be produced and distributed efficiently in a centralized fashion (King and Cordeiro-Guerra 2005; Montreal Economic Institute 2007). Hanushek and Woessmann (2007) suggest that most of the incentives that affect learning outcomes are institutional in nature. They identify three incentives in particular: (1) choice and competition, (2) school autonomy, and (3) school accountability. The idea behind choice and competition is that parents who are interested in maximizing their children's learning outcomes are able to choose to send their children to the most productive school (productive in terms of academic results) that they can find. This demand-side pressure will give all schools an incentive to improve their performance if they want to compete for students. Similarly, local decision making and fiscal decentralization can have positive effects on outcomes such as test scores or graduation rates by holding the schools accountable for the "output" they produce. *World Development Report 2004: Making Services Work for Poor People* (*WDR 2004*) presents a very similar framework in that it suggests that good quality and timely service provision can be ensured if service providers can be held accountable to their *clients* (World Bank 2003). In the case of the education sector, the clients would be students and their parents.

In some countries (mostly developed and some developing ones), the core idea behind SBM is that those who work in a school building should have greater management control of what goes on in the building. In other countries (mostly developing ones), the idea behind SBM is less ambitious, focusing mainly on involving community members and parents in the school decision-making process rather than putting them entirely in control. In both cases, however, the central government always plays some role in education, and the precise definition of this role affects how SBM activities are conceived and implemented.

SBM in almost all of its manifestations involves community members in school decision making. Because these community members usually are parents of children enrolled in the school, they have an incentive to improve their children's education. As a result, SBM can be expected to improve student achievement and other outcomes because these local people demand closer monitoring of school personnel, better student evaluations, a closer match between the school's needs and its policies, and a more efficient use of resources. For instance, although the evidence is mixed, it appears that in a number of diverse countries (such as India, Nicaragua, and Papua New Guinea), parental participation in school management has reduced teacher absenteeism.[1]

SBM has several other benefits. Under these arrangements, schools are managed more transparently, and that reduces opportunities for corruption. Also, SBM often gives parents and stakeholders opportunities to increase their skills. In some cases, training in shared decision making, interpersonal relations, and management skills is offered to school council members so that they may become more capable participants in the SBM process (Briggs and Wohlstetter 1999) and may benefit the community as a whole.

## A Typology of School-Based Management

SBM has been introduced in economies whose educational systems are quite dissimilar: El Salvador, Guatemala, Hong Kong, China, Indonesia, Israel, Kenya, the Netherlands, New Zealand, Nicaragua, Niger, Qatar, Thailand, the United Kingdom, the United States, and many others. These SBM reforms have been far from uniform, however, and they have encompassed a wide variety of different approaches. As the definition of SBM reflects, it is a form of decentralization that makes the school the centerpiece of educational improvement and relies on the redistribution of responsibilities as the primary way to bring about that improvement. This definition leaves plenty of room for interpretation, and the reality is

**Table 1.1 Various Functions for Which Responsibility Is Devolved to School Councils, Selected Countries**

| Council Function | Benin | The Gambia | Ghana | FPESP, Kenya | FAF, Madagascar | FRAM, Madagascar | DSSP, Mozambique | COGES, Niger | Qatar | Rwanda | Senegal |
|---|---|---|---|---|---|---|---|---|---|---|---|
| **Personnel management** | | | | | | | | | | | |
| Paying staff salaries | | + | | | | | | | * | | |
| Establishing incentives for teaching staff | * | * | | | * | * | | | * | | |
| Hiring/firing teaching staff | | | | | | * | | + | * | | |
| Hiring/firing administrative staff | | * | | | | * | | + | * | | |
| Supervising and evaluating teachers | | * | | | | | | * | * | | |
| Funding teacher training | * | * | | | * | * | | | * | | * |
| **Pedagogy** | | | | | | | | | | | |
| Setting classroom hours by subject | | * | | | | | | | * | | |
| Selecting some text-books/curriculum | | + | | * | * | | | | * | | |
| Setting the method of instruction | | * | | | | | | | * | | |
| Setting the school calendar | . | | | | | | | | | | |

**Maintenance and infrastructure**

Building/maintaining school

Buying school materials

**Budget**

Overseeing budget

Allocating budget

Establishing school fee

**Monitoring and evaluation**

Conducting administrative activities

Making pedagogical decisions

*Source:* Adapted from di Gropello (2006).

*Note:* COGES = school management committee; DSSP = Devolved Social Services Program; FAF = Association of Teachers; FPESP = Primary Education Support Program; FRAM = Association of Parents of School Children.

* = full responsibility; + = some responsibility.

that there are now many different kinds of SBM being implemented. SBM reforms are shaped by the reformers' objectives and by broader national policy and social contexts.

SBM approaches differ in two main ways—the "who" (to whom the decision-making authority is devolved) and the "what" (the degree of autonomy that is devolved). These factors are what we call the autonomy-participation nexus. The various combinations of these two dimensions make almost every SBM reform unique. The Southwest Educational Development Laboratory (http://www.sedl.org) in the United States has an inventory of more than 800 SBM models (Rowan, Camburn, and Barnes 2004), and about 29 of them have been evaluated at least once (Borman et al. 2003). Cook (2007) explains SBM as a construct of modest "entitivity"—in other words, a model that cannot have a unique form in all of the places in which it is implemented (see box 1.1), which means that SBM reforms around the world are inevitably different from each other. In the discussion that follows, we explore the main forms taken by SBM, but the discussion by no means presents an exhaustive typology.

### The Autonomy Continuum

SBM programs lie along a continuum of the degree to which decision making is devolved to the local level—from limited autonomy, to more ambitious programs that allow schools to hire and fire teachers, to programs that give schools control over substantial resources, to those that promote private and community management of schools, and finally to those that eventually may allow parents to create their own schools. Figure 1.1 depicts this "weak"-to-"strong" continuum and positions some of the countries that have implemented SBM reforms along it. Note, however, that we do not use the terms "weak" or "strong" to classify any SBM system as better or worse than any other system. Rather, we use the terms simply to define the degree of autonomy awarded to the school level. For instance, we define "weak" SBM reforms as those in which schools have only limited autonomy, usually over areas related to instructional methods or planning for school improvement (as in Mexico) (Karim, Santizo Rodall, and Cabrero Mendoza 2004; Skoufias and Shapiro 2006).

When school councils start serving an advisory role, as in Prince William County in Virginia (Drury and Levin 1994) or in Edmonton, Canada (Wohlstetter and Mohrman 1996; Abu-Duhou 1999), the

**Box 1.1**

# The Modest "Entivity" of School-Based Management

In 1999, the United States Congress passed a comprehensive school reform act that outlined the 11 components of an autonomous local school. However, a school may be thought to have adopted either comprehensive school reform or school-based management (SBM) without every one of those 11 components in place. No one has specified a minimum or core number of attributes needed for a school to qualify for either label. But it is obvious that the more components included in an SBM plan, the more radical the organizational change. To varying degrees in the United States, schools can and do choose among these components. Depending on the school, one component may be either central or peripheral to the school's strategic plan; and that component may be put into practice as its inventor intended or may be adapted in ways that the inventor would not recognize or like. Given all of the possible combinations of these components, it is clear that there are thousands of different ways to put together an SBM plan, and how this is done may have important consequences for the school and for the reform as a whole.

A school may choose to make fundamental changes to all of its administrative, pedagogical, and external relations functions or to change only a few of them. The key decision-making authority may stay with the principal; be shared with teachers; or be shared with teachers, parents, and other community representatives. As their major goal, the new decision makers might choose to modify the curriculum, to improve students' social behavior, improve students' academic performance, reduce teacher turnover—or all of the above. Performance monitoring may be central, peripheral, or nonexistent; and if it exists, it may require quantitative data or simply informal feedback. Parents may be asked to perform many school roles or be involved only tangentially; and there may be many parents involved or just a few.

The point is not merely that each of the 11 components may be made operational in multiple ways, but also that each component may be combined in thousands of ways across all of the variants of all of the other components. The net result is that, whatever the achieved theoretical consensus about SBM, it still has modest "entivity" because the core concept always may be indexed as the degree to which change occurs in the locus of decision making favoring the whole-school level. However, the context in which SBM is put into practice is so variable that one school's SBM is unlikely to look like that of another.

*Source:* Cook 2007.

**Figure 1.1 Classification of School-Based Management Reforms Implemented in Various Economies**

| Weak | Moderate | Somewhat strong | Strong | Very strong[1] |
|---|---|---|---|---|
| Limited autonomy over school affairs, mainly for planning and instruction | School councils have been established, but serve only an advisory role | Councils have autonomy to hire and fire teachers and principals and to set curricula | ...and control substantial resources (for example, lump-sum funding) | Parental or community control of schools | ...and any choice of models, in which parents or others can create a school |

| | | | | | |
|---|---|---|---|---|---|
| Czech Republic<br>Mexico | Brazil<br>Canada<br>Thailand<br>Virginia, USA | Chicago, USA<br>New York, USA<br>Spain<br>United Kingdom (LM) | Australia<br>El Salvador<br>Guatemala<br>Ghana<br>Honduras<br>Hong Kong, China<br>Madagascar<br>New Zealand<br>Nicaragua<br>Rwanda | Niger<br>United Kingdom (GM) | Denmark<br>Netherlands<br>Qatar |
| | Florida, USA | The Gambia | | | |
| | Benin<br>Cambodia<br>Indonesia<br>Israel<br>Kenya<br>Mozambique<br>Senegal | | | | |

*Source:* Authors' compilation from the literature.

*Note:* For the United Kingdom, LM = locally managed schools, and GM = grant-maintained schools, two slightly different school-based management models implemented there.

1. These terms represent ratings in the continuum of autonomy and authority vested in schools by the various types of SBM reforms.

reform can be classified as "moderate." As these councils become more autonomous—receiving funds directly from the central or other relevant level of government (for example, lump-sum funding or grants), hiring and firing teachers and principals, and setting curricula—the reform is a much stronger type of SBM. Schools like those can be found in El Salvador (di Gropello 2006) and New Zealand (Wylie 1996). At the "very strong" end of the continuum are local public education systems in which parents have complete choice and control over all educational decisions; where schools are stand-alone units; and where all decisions concerning schools' operational, financial, and educational management are made by the school councils or school administrators. In these cases, parents or any other community members may even establish fully autonomous, publicly funded private schools, as in Denmark and the Netherlands; and, in a few cases, fully autonomous public (charter) schools, as in the United Kingdom and some U.S. states (Abu-Duhou 1999). It is interesting to note that, to some extent, parents have a similar degree of autonomy and choice in both private schools and publicly funded, fully autonomous schools.

### The Autonomy-Participation Nexus

In addition to the "what" dimension (the degree of devolved autonomy), we have the "who" dimension. Who gets the decision-making power when it is devolved to the school level? In a simple world, the following four models would be sufficient to define who is invested with decision-making power in any SBM reform (Leithwood and Menzies 1998):

1. *Administrative-control SBM* devolves authority to the school principal. This model aims to make each school more accountable to the central district or board office. The benefits of this kind of SBM include increasing the efficiency of expenditures on personnel and curriculum and making one person at each school more accountable to the central authority.

2. *Professional-control SBM* devolves the main decision-making authority to teachers. This model aims to make better use of teachers' knowledge of what the school needs at the classroom level. Participating fully in the decision-making process also may motivate teachers to perform better and may lead to greater efficiency and effectiveness in teaching.

3. *Community-control SBM* devolves the main decision-making authority to parents or the community. Under this model, teachers and
   principals are assumed to become more responsive to parents' needs.
   Another benefit is that the curriculum can reflect local needs and
   preferences.
4. *Balanced-control SBM* balances decision-making authority between
   parents and teachers, the two main stakeholders in any school. Its aims
   are to take advantage of teachers' detailed knowledge of the school to
   improve school management and to make schools more accountable
   to parents.

But, of course, things are not as simple as all that. The administrative control model never can exist in its pure form because principals
never can operate on their own in practice. Principals need other people to work for them and to help them make decisions for the school.
Existing models of SBM around the world generally blend the four
models described above. In most cases, power is devolved to a formal
legal entity—a school council or school management committee—that
consists of teachers as well as the principal. In nearly all versions of
SBM, community representatives also serve on the council or committee. As a result, school personnel get to know the local people to whom
they ultimately are accountable and so are more likely to take local
needs and wishes into account when making decisions, realizing that
local residents are able to monitor what the school professionals are
doing. Although community involvement may improve program planning and implementation in these ways, school personnel occasionally
involve community members only superficially in a way that does not
complicate the lives of principals and teachers (Cook 2007). Although
parents and community members have roles to play in SBM, those
roles are not universally clear and not always central. In some cases, the
legal entity that has the main authority to implement SBM is a parents'
council, but it cannot operate successfully without the support of the
teachers and the principal.

The autonomy-participation nexus defines the essence of an SBM
reform: who gets what and how much of it. Figure 1.2 uses a few of the
more popular SBM reforms around the world to illustrate this nexus. For
example, the AGEs program in Mexico gives minimal autonomy to school
councils, which are run mainly by parents (Gertler, Rubio-Codina, and
Patrinos 2006). Thus, in figure 1.2 that program lies low on the y-axis (low

**Figure 1.2    The Autonomy-Participation Nexus, Selected Countries**

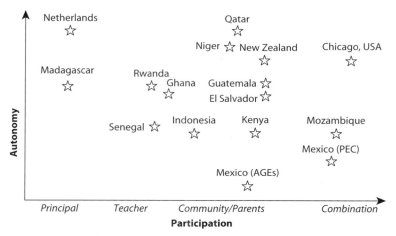

*Source:* Authors' compilation from the literature.

autonomy) and along the x-axis at the point where parents and the community receive the authority that is devolved. New Zealand is another matter, as can be seen in the figure. SBM there is highly autonomous, with most of the decision-making power lying with parents, so New Zealand rests high on the y-axis and in roughly the same x-axis position as Mexico (Wylie 1996). The Netherlands is another extreme. In 1985 it devolved decision-making power to school principals to make schools more efficient. Parents in the Netherlands can create new schools that meet their own specific cultural and religious needs. The U.S. city Chicago is a good example of a school system in which combinations of community members, teachers, and principals were given a high level of autonomy (Cook, Hunt, and Murphy 2000).

## *The Autonomy-Participation-Accountability Nexus*

There is another link in the autonomy-participation chain—accountability. In a number of countries, one of the main objectives of introducing SBM is to make schools more accountable and their management more transparent. Anderson (2005) has suggested that there are three types of accountability in SBM. Those who run schools must be (1) accountable for adhering to rules and accountable to the education authorities, (2) accountable for adhering to standards and accountable to their peers, and (3) accountable for student learning and accountable to the general public. SBM programs both strengthen and simplify these types of account-ability by empowering people at the school level to make decisions collectively, thus increasing the transparency of the process. Consequently, students' learning achievement and other outcomes can be expected to improve because stakeholders at the school level can monitor school personnel, work to improve student evaluations, ensure a closer match between school needs and policies, and use resources more efficiently.

By increasing transparency, SBM also can reduce corruption. For instance, the limited autonomy form of SBM in Mexico's PEC has been credited with preventing and limiting corrupt practices in the manage-ment of educational funds (Karim, Santizo Rodall, and Cabrero Mendoza 2004) because the school councils are accountable both to their central education authorities (vertical accountability) and to the school community and donors (horizontal accountability). If expanded, this program has the potential to reduce petty corruption, as docu-mented by Transparency International (2005) and Patrinos and Kagia (2007). Table 1.2 shows that a number of economies have introduced SBM with the explicit goal of increasing accountability and community and parental participation in the decision-making process. The account-ability aspect of SBM reforms also has been highlighted in the *WDR 2004* (World Bank 2003) as a way to strengthen accountability rela-tionships between the clients (parents and students) and the service providers (teachers, principals, and the government).

By its very nature, SBM has the potential to hold school-level decision makers accountable for their actions. But in many countries it may be necessary to build the capacity of community members, teachers, and principals to create or augment a culture of accountability.

## Toward a Conceptual Framework for Analyzing School-Based Management

A conceptual framework by which SBM can be analyzed may be pre-sented in the messages in the *WDR 2004* (World Bank 2003), which present evidence that increasing school autonomy and accountability can help solve some of the most fundamental problems in education. According to that evidence, although increasing resource flows and other support to the education sector is necessary to give poor people greater access to quality education, in no way is that sufficient. It also is necessary to translate those resources into basic services that are accessible to the poor. Therefore, schools should be given some autonomy over the use of

**Table 1.2  Selective List of Economies with School-Based Management Reforms**

| Economy | Date first implemented | Objectives of/Motivation for reform | Type of SBM[a] |
|---|---|---|---|
| Australia | 1970s | Increase efficiency through near-total autonomy | Strong |
| Canada | 1970s (Edmonton), 1996 (Ontario) | Increase parental and community participation in education and grant schools more autonomy | Moderate |
| United States (Florida; Chicago, Illinois; New York; Virginia; and others) | 1970s and 1980s | Most reforms sought to increase efficiency, empower teachers, and involve the community in schools; some reforms (such as in Chicago) made improving student achievement an explicit objective | Moderate to somewhat strong |
| Brazil | 1982 | Increase efficiency in school management, create more democratic and meritocratic process for electing school personnel, and increase community and parent participation | Moderate |
| Spain | 1985 | Democratize education | Somewhat strong |
| United Kingdom | 1988 | Give schools financial autonomy and increase school effectiveness | Strong |
| New Zealand | 1990 | Increase community autonomy and efficiency | Strong |
| El Salvador | 1991 | Increase access in rural areas, encourage community participation, and improve quality of schooling | Strong |
| Hong Kong, China | 1991 | Increase accountability, participatory decision making, and school effectiveness | Strong |
| Nicaragua | 1991 | Increase community participation, obtain financial resources beyond government funding, and increase efficiency | Strong |
| Netherlands | 1992 | Empower school principals in order to increase efficiency | Very strong |
| Czech Republic | 1993 | Make system more open, flexible, and democratic | Moderate |
| Ghana | 1995 | Increase involvement of school management committees to increase accountability in the use of capitation grants | Somewhat strong in theory; weak in practice |

*(continued)*

27

**Table 1.2  Selective List of Economies with School-Based Management Reforms** (*Continued*)

| Economy | Date first implemented | Objectives of/Motivation for reform | Type of SBM[a] |
|---|---|---|---|
| Guatemala | 1996 | Increase access, decentralize educational decision making, increase community participation, and maintain linguistic diversity | Strong |
| Mexico (AGEs) | 1996 | Increase parental participation in rural schools | Moderate |
| Israel | 1997 | Improve public school system, school management, monitoring, and assessment | Somewhat strong |
| Mozambique | 1997 | Increase access to higher-quality education through decentralized management and budget allocations | Moderate |
| Thailand | 1997 | Improve quality of education and increase the country's competitiveness | Somewhat strong |
| Cambodia | 1998 | Improve education | Somewhat strong |
| Honduras | 1999 | Increase access in rural areas and encourage community participation | Strong |
| Mexico (PEC) | 2001 | Improve educational quality by granting more autonomy to schools | Moderate |
| Madagascar | 2002 | Improve education | Somewhat strong |
| Niger | 2002 | Increase access to education by reducing school fees, support decentralization, send money directly to the school management committee to spend, and empower local communities to participate in decision making with the head teacher | Strong |
| Kenya | 2003 | Increase accountability of schools and teachers by improving incentives and improve school management | Moderate |

| Country | Year | Description | Rating |
|---|---|---|---|
| Qatar | 2003 | Generate a variety of schooling alternatives to improve education, decentralize the schooling system, and increase accountability | Strong |
| Indonesia | 2005 | Increase accountability and responsiveness to parents and students and enhance the role of school committees | Moderate |
| Rwanda | 2005 | Identify hiring practices for contract teachers and increase the involvement of PTAs in school management to enhance governance at the school level | Somewhat strong |
| Benin | 2006 | Increase the decision-making power of school councils and newly elected municipal councils, increase parent participation, and encourage transparent financial management | Moderate |
| Gambia, The | 2008 | Improve teaching and learning of the pupils; raise awareness about the interconnectedness of various factors affecting student learning; and increase coordination among school administration, the students' parents, and other stakeholders | Moderate |
| Senegal | 2008 | Improve teachers' training | Moderate |

*Source:* Authors' compilation from the literature.

*Note:* PTA = parent-teacher association; SBM = school-based management.

a. The classification of types of SBM is as follows: *Very strong* = full or almost full control of schools by councils, parents, or school administrators; full choice via the possibility of creating new public schools (that is, charter schools). *Strong* = high degree of autonomy given to school councils over budget and staffing (that is, schools receive lump-sum funding or grants). *Somewhat strong* = councils have authority to hire and fire teachers and/or principals and to set curricula, but have more limited autonomy regarding finances and control of resources. *Moderate* = school councils have been established but they serve mainly an advisory role or have limited autonomy for planning and strategic purposes. *Weak* = the public school system is decentralized to the municipal or regional level, but schools have virtually no autonomy to make any administrative or curricular decisions.

their inputs and should be held accountable to their clients for employing these inputs efficiently. The theoretical literature that promotes using SBM recommends four tenets for improving service delivery to the poor: (1) increasing poor people's opportunity to choose schools and participate, (2) giving citizens a stronger voice, (3) making information about schools' performance widely available, and (4) strengthening the rewards given to schools that deliver effective services to the poor and penalizing those that fail to deliver (Barnett 1996).

The *WDR 2004* framework for analyzing the provision of education services defines four aspects of accountability:

1. *voice*—how well citizens can hold politicians and policy makers accountable for their performance in discharging their responsibility to provide education
2. *compacts*—how well and how clearly the responsibilities and objectives of public education policy are communicated
3. *management*—the actions that develop effective front-line providers within organizations
4. *client power*—how well citizens, as clients, can increase the accountability of schools and school systems.

In the words of the *WDR 2004*, effective solutions are likely to involve a mixture of voice, choice, direct participation, and organizational command and control (World Bank 2003). The report goes on to suggest that the key element shared by successful education systems is a meaningful accountability system. Figure 1.3 presents the *WDR 2004* framework as a three-cornered relationship among citizens, politicians, and service providers. When the public sector is involved in service delivery, the accountability mechanism works through two key relationships—compact and voice. This is called the long route of accountability in the WDR framework (figure 1.3). The short route of accountability is when the providers are accountable directly to the clients by passing decisions and powers directly to the citizens or communities. The service provision and accountability relationships among these actors are complex: even within each group of actors, there usually are heterogeneous subgroups, and the incentives and accountability relationships that work for one group may differ from those that work for other groups. When accountability fails, the failure can be tracked either to the long route or to the short route. Sometimes improving the long route is a long-term process and, in some situations, may not be feasible. In such cases, the *WDR 2004* suggests

**Figure 1.3** *World Development Report 2004* **Accountability Framework**

Long route of accountability

The state
Politicians | Policy makers

Voice

Compact

Citizens/clients
Nonpoor | Poor

Short route

Client power

Providers
Frontline | Organization

Services

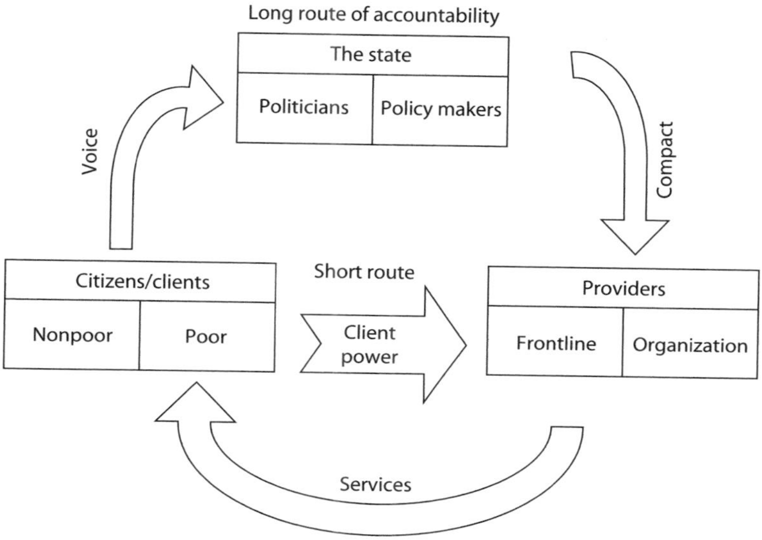

*Source:* World Bank 2003.

**Figure 1.4 School-Based Management Accountability Framework**

Long route of accountability

The state
Politicians | Policy makers

Voice

Compact

Citizens/clients
Nonpoor | Poor

Client power
Management

Providers
Frontline | Organization

Client power
Management

Services

School committee
Clients | Providers

Short route of accountability

*Source:* Authors' illustration.

strengthening the short route in which the service providers are held directly accountable to the citizens or clients. The clients can improve service delivery by (1) using their voice to ensure that services are tailored to their needs and (2) monitoring the providers. In cases where short-route improvements already are being tested and/or where society is amenable to long-route improvements, long-route improvements should be adopted.

Theoretically, SBM models encompass all of the four relationships of accountability envisaged in the *WDR 2004*. The term *compact* refers to the long route of accountability, whereby the central government delegates responsibility to the line ministries, which then delegate to schools the responsibility to perform various tasks. From that perspective, in certain models of SBM the accountability of school principals is upward, to the ministry that holds them responsible for providing services to the clients who, in turn, have put the policy makers in power and thus have the *voice* to hold the policy makers and politicians accountable for their performance. In most cases of SBM, the *management mechanisms* change under reforms—the clients themselves become part of the management, along with the front-line providers. Thus, the short route of accountability becomes even shorter as representatives of the clients—either parents or community members—get the authority to make certain decisions and have a voice in decisions that directly affect the students who attend the school. The SBM framework is presented in figure 1.4, where the school manager, whether the principal alone or a committee of parents and teachers, acts as the accountable entity.

Thus, SBM can be a way of ensuring accountability and autonomy as envisaged in the *WDR 2004*, but with an added group of agents—the school managers (in other words, the group to whom the autonomy is devolved). This group usually consists of a partnership of the various agents who can hold each other accountable while providing the services needed by the school in question. How successful this additional group of agents has been as the repository of devolved authority for running schools has not been established.

## How School-Based Management Can Increase Participation and Improve School Outcomes

In developed countries, SBM is introduced explicitly to improve students' academic performance. But in developing countries, how school decentralization eventually will affect student performance is less clear.

This section tries to define the ways in which SBM can increase participation and transparency and improve school outcomes.

First, the SBM model must define exactly which powers are vested in which individuals or committees, and how these powers are to be coordinated to make the plan workable within both the school culture and the available resources. However, the structure of authority needs to remain flexible enough to enable school managers to deal with any unexpected events (events that always seem to emerge during implementation).

Second, the success of SBM requires the support of the various school-level stakeholders, particularly teachers (Cook 2007). Also vital to that success is the school principals' support of the decentralization reform (De Grauwe 2005). That support is not a foregone conclusion because principals will remain personally accountable for the performance of their school, but no longer will have complete control over its management. In effect, they are being asked to give up some authority without a corresponding decrease in personal accountability. When SBM is in place, principals no longer may blame the policies of the school district when things go wrong. The support of both local and national governments is required as well. By definition, SBM requires these governments to surrender some power and authority to the school level, but they retain the right and ability to reverse their earlier decision in favor of SBM if they feel their power is being usurped.

The final and most important source of required support is parents and other community leaders. It is necessary, however, to distinguish between parents and other community members. Whereas parents always are part of the community that surrounds a school, school councils do not have to include parents as members. In the United States, for instance, many schools are controlled locally in the sense that a school board of local residents officially sets policy, but it is possible that none of the students' parents will be members of that board. In some cases, wealthy individuals in a community may be members of a school council simply because they support the school financially.

Particularly in developed countries, parental participation as members of school councils or of the group that is implementing SBM is distinct from community participation. In developing countries, particularly in isolated small or rural communities, however, parental participation tends to be synonymous with community participation because almost everybody in these small communities has a family member in school.

The expectation underlying SBM is that greater parent involvement will mean that schools are more responsive to local demands (for example, demands for better teaching methods or more inputs), and that decisions will be made in the interest of children rather than of adults. A further hope is that involved parents will become unpaid or minimally paid auxiliary staff who help teachers in classrooms and assist with other minor activities (as happens, for instance, in the AGEs program in Mexico). Furthermore, even if parents are too busy working to help in the classroom, they still can encourage their children to do their homework and can show them in other ways that the family really values schooling and academic achievement. Because parents are networked in various ways with community leaders, it is also hoped that parental support for SBM will encourage local community leaders to put schools higher on their political agendas and thus provide the schools with more material resources.

When the nexus of autonomy-participation-accountability has been defined and a realistic management plan has been drawn up and has the support of all stakeholders, then it becomes possible to expect better school outcomes. Thereafter, the hope is that the school climate will change as the stakeholders work together in a collegial way to manage the school. However, there is little evidence that this really happens in practice. Also, the possibility exists that teachers and principals will come to resent being monitored constantly by parents and school council members, and that resentment will cause relationships within the school to deteriorate.

At the same time, a school's teaching climate is predicated on how motivated teachers are to teach well, whether they know how to teach well, how good the various curricula are, how eager pupils are to learn, and how much parents actually support their children's learning in whatever ways are practical for them. Any school that wants to improve its academic record will have to work actively on some or all of those factors. Sometimes the obstacles to improving the quality of instruction are motivational, sometimes they are cognitive (that is, they involve what teachers do and do not know), and sometimes they are social (petty personal matters that can prevent teachers from behaving professionally). Ideally, because people who run the school are intimately acquainted with the individuals who work there, they will be able to identify the specific problems that need to be fixed and use their authority to find and implement solutions.

Some caveats about SBM must be mentioned. Decentralization or devolution does not necessarily give more power to the general public because the power devolved by the reform is susceptible to capture by elites. As for the relationship between decentralization, pro-poor growth, and reduced corruption, the evidence is mixed (see Alderman 1998; Faguet 2001; and Fisman and Gatti 2002). Bardhan and Mookherjee (2000, 2006) and Bardhan (2002) suggest that there may be numerous reasons why local control over resource allocation or decision making does not yield the desired outcomes.

First, local democracy and political accountability often are weak in developing countries and can lead to elite groups capturing governance at the various levels. Such capture may occur even in well-established democracies. For example, the transfer of school management authority in Chicago, Illinois, was made to each school's local school council, composed of the principal, teacher representatives, parents, and local community members. In some cases, the local community members organized to take over one or more school councils and then used the councils for their own political ends rather than for the better education of children. Because those ends included more community control over city resources and a greater say over noneducational matters, the mayor of Chicago ended the SBM experiment, reclaiming authority and budgets and thus essentially gutting the local school councils (Cook 2007). This example further suggests that the SBM reforms must be supported not only by parents, teachers, and community members, but also by local or national governments. To transfer power to schools is to transfer it from somewhere else, and the entity that is losing some of its power often is in a position to reverse its earlier decision if the reform contravenes its original intent. Government support for SBM is highly desirable, and indifference is tolerable so long as the government money continues to flow. However, opposition is a constant source of worry to principals and other school leaders (Cook 2007).

Second, in more traditional and rural areas with a history of feudalism, sometimes the poor or minorities feel the need for a strong central authority to ensure that they are able to access services in the same way as more powerful local citizens access them. In a related vein, there may be no culture of accountability within communities, no one who would think to question any actions taken by the group running the school (De Grauwe 2005). That situation can be a problem in places where the teacher is regarded as the ultimate authority by virtue of being the only highly educated person in a community. And last, those people who are given the responsibility for managing the school may not have the capacity to do so, which points up the need to build the capacity of education stakeholders at the grassroots level to ensure that SBM reforms do not fail in their execution.

Third, during the implementing of SBM reforms, challenges often arise that can undermine the reforms' potential success. In the United States, for example, in implementing the Comer's School Development Program (SDP) in Detroit, Michigan, school planning and management teams were set up in each school. The teams comprised the principal, teachers' representatives, and representatives of parents and other community members. After four years, program evaluators concluded that only 4 of 12 schools achieved satisfactory levels of implementation (Cook 2007, p. 12). The same (or a smaller) fraction achieved satisfactory levels in Prince George's County, Virginia, and in Chicago. Most shortfalls in implementation were attributed to the following factors: (1) new principals entering the school and preferring different kinds of reform of their own choosing; (2) established principals realizing that the reform required them to devolve authority to others while the school district held them alone accountable for changes in the school's performance; (3) initial disharmony existing among teachers who did not want the reform package the district or principal was offering them; (4) teachers realizing that the reforms meant more work for them, including some work prompted by parents being involved more directly in the reform; (5) parents being unable to find the time to go to the school more often and generally not feeling comfortable interacting with teachers whose technical jargon sometimes was not understood even by native English speakers; and (6) the level of school district support for the program waxing and waning as district priorities changed. Above all, little can be achieved by SBM unless teachers want to and know how to change their teaching behavior when their classroom doors close. A minority of schools overcame these obstacles, but most could not (Cook 2007).[2]

These caveats help strengthen our understanding of the pattern of SBM in developing countries (as discussed above). In particular, the caveats strengthen the notion that the specific type of SBM introduced in any given country depends (or should depend) on the political economy of the particular country. For instance, strong SBM reforms have been introduced, and have been quite successful, in those countries where communities have been forced by some calamity such as war or a natural disaster to come together as a group to find ways to deliver basic services, including education.

## Notes

1. For a detailed discussion, see Karim, Santizo Rodall, and Cabrero Mendoza (2004) and Patrinos and Kagia (2007).

2. Cook (2007) argues that it is not yet clear whether these shortfalls result from program features that can be fixed easily or from features intrinsic to the SDP model, and so cannot be remedied easily. An overall judgment about the potential of SDP depends heavily on how one decides this last issue.

CHAPTER 2

# School-Based Management Reforms around the World

This chapter describes in more detail SBM reforms around the world. We focus on four regions—Latin America and the Caribbean, Africa, Asia, and the Middle East and North Africa—and several countries in other parts of the world. In the case of each region, we briefly describe the types of SBM programs in the countries studied and the effects of the SBM reforms. Those effects are grouped into five main categories: (1) effects on access (coverage), (2) effects on student test scores, (3) effects on internal efficiency indicators (dropout, failure, and repetition rates), (4) effects on parental and community involvement, and (5) effects on other indicators.

## General Assessment of the Literature on School-Based Management Programs around the World

One general conclusion is that the sample of carefully documented, rigorous impact evaluations of SBM since 1995 is very small, given the large number of known SBM programs that exist around the world. This situation is changing, with various rigorous evaluations under way in countries in Africa and Asia. However, at this time we know little about the effects of SBM. Moreover, most of the studies reviewed here used empirical strategies that are open to question.

Nonetheless, the studies that do exist represent an important effort to quantify the impact of some SBM programs on educational outcomes. It can be argued that they have reduced the bias that undoubtedly is present in simple comparisons and in that way have made advanced our understanding of the effect of SBM policies.

Although it is very difficult to establish the sizes of the outcome variables of interest because of the different metrics used in the various studies, it is possible to list some findings about the impact of SBM, based on the more rigorous analyses:

1. Some studies found that SBM policies actually changed the dynamics of the school, either because parents got more involved or because teachers' actions changed (King and Özler 1998; Jimenez and Sawada 1999; Gunnarsson et al. 2004; Duflo, Dupas, and Kremer 2007).
2. Several studies presented evidence of SBM's positive impact on reducing repetition; failure; and, to a lesser degree, dropout rates (Paes de Barros and Mendonça 1998; Jimenez and Sawada 2003; di Gropello and Marshall 2005; Gertler, Rubio-Codina, and Patrinos 2006; Skoufias and Shapiro 2006).
3. The studies that had access to standardized test scores presented mixed evidence, with countries such as El Salvador, Kenya, Mexico, and Nicaragua showing positive results (King and Özler 1998; Jimenez and Sawada 2003; Sawada and Ragatz 2005; Lopez-Calva and Espinosa 2006). One of the studies showing strong positive evidence was the randomized experiment in Kenya, where an SBM initiative implemented in randomly selected schools had large positive effects on student test scores. These effects were the result of a combination of smaller class sizes, more teacher incentives, and greater parental oversight (Duflo, Dupas, and Kremer 2007). Other reforms, such as those in Brazil and Honduras, appear to have had no effect on test scores.

The general finding that SBM shows positive results on some variables (mainly in reducing repetition and failure and improving teacher attendance rates), contrasted with the mixed results in test scores, may have been prompted by the timing and strength of the particular SBM reforms. Research in the United States suggests that, in general, an SBM reform must have been in operation for about 5 years before any fundamental changes are seen at the school level; only after 8 years of implementation can changes be seen in more difficult-to-modify indicators, such as test scores. Moreover, it is possible to argue that school learning is a cumulative process and that students must be exposed to the reform for a longer period of time to enjoy its potential benefits.

Three studies (Paes de Barros and Mendonça 1998; Parker 2005; and Lopez-Calva and Espinosa 2006) allowed at least 8 years to pass before measuring the effects of the intervention on test scores. Paes de Barros and Mendonça found that the reform in Brazil had produced no test score improvements after 11 years of implementation, but the other two studies showed that the reforms in Mexico and Nicaragua had positive effects on test scores after 8 and 11 years, respectively. The results from Kenya underscore the possibility of obtaining positive results on student learning from combining more resources (extra teachers, in that case) with SBM initiatives (Duflo, Dupas, and Kremer 2007). Other studies measured SBM's impact on repetition and failure rates (intermediate indicators) closer to the initial implementation period. The authors of those studies found positive effects after only 2 years of implementation in the case of rural Mexico (Gertler, Rubio-Codina, and Patrinos 2006) and after only 3 years in urban Mexico (Skoufias and Shapiro 2006).

The lack of cost-benefit analyses of SBM is another important gap in the literature. Clearly, SBM is a very inexpensive initiative because it constitutes a change only in the locus of decision making and not necessarily in the amount of resources invested in the system. If the few positive impact evaluations are true, then SBM can be regarded as a very cost-effective initiative.

Rigorous evaluations of many SBM reforms around the world are planned or already under way, including ones in Benin, Ghana, Indonesia, Madagascar, Mozambique, and Rwanda. Evidence from these new studies will shed light on SBM reform and in a few years will yield more conclusive evidence regarding its effects.

## Initiatives in Latin America and the Caribbean

In this section we review each country's experience with SBM, providing a brief description of the country's SBM reform and a review of the evidence on the five categories of effects listed above.

### Brazil

Beginning in 1982, several states in Brazil experimented with varying forms and degrees of SBM. Three key innovations stand out in the Brazilian experience with SBM: (1) schools have been given financial autonomy; (2) principals are elected democratically by school officials, parents, and students or are competitively appointed by local governments via examinations (or a combination of both); and (3) councils are established in the schools to coordinate and evaluate the schools' pedagogical, administrative, and financial activities. The school councils comprise the principal, representatives of teachers and other staff, and representatives of parents and students. Only four states implemented all three reforms in a coordinated way—Minas Gerais, Rio Grande do Norte, Espirito Santo, and Mato Grosso do Sul (Paes de Barros and Mendonça 1998).

Paes de Barros and Mendonça used census, household survey, and evaluation data from the National Basic Education System to carry out an empirical investigation into the effects of the three SBM innovations on student achievement. They measured the effects by assessing students' average performance in mathematics, language, and science in grades 1, 3, 5, and 7 in each school (test scores are averaged at the school level because not all grades are examined in these three subjects). The authors included such control variables as mean per capita family income, average teacher quality, and average educational attainment. The unit of analysis was the state, and the time period for the study was 1981–93 (although some analyses used fewer years because of data restrictions). The authors' empirical strategy was to compare states' performance on various outcomes by using each state's time variation in implementing innovations. Their results suggest that the financial autonomy reforms did not lead to better student performance (Paes de Barros and Mendonça 1998).

Another set of SBM reforms began in 1998, and by 2001 it had reached more than 5,600 schools. These reforms, known as the PDE, were designed to make schools more responsive to students and their communities. Under PDE, schools engage in a self-evaluation, develop a school plan focusing on two or three "efficiency factors" (one of which has to be effective teaching and learning), and design actions to enhance them. A program created by the Ministry of Education to strengthen the schools—Fundescola—provides funds to support the goals and projects of PDE schools (Carnoy et al. 2008).

Carnoy et al.'s evaluation of the PDE found that, although the program did affect what went on in schools (in terms of such activities as planning, participation of parent-teacher associations, and suitable working conditions for teachers), it did not appear to have any significant effect on Portuguese language and mathematics test scores. Within all PDE schools, however, those schools that received more funds did appear to improve their test scores more than did those receiving fewer funds. Of all the spending categories, spending on learning materials and on school furniture appears to have had the greatest effects on learning.

Conroy et al. used a rich longitudinal data set covering 1999–2002, which included PDE schools and a matched set of non-PDE schools. The authors' multivariate analysis approach controlled for preexisting differences across schools in PDE exposure, individual and family characteristics, teacher and school characteristics, and parents' selection of schools. This last variable was used to address concerns that sample (program) selection might bias the results.

When studying the effects of the Brazilian reforms on dropout, failure, and repetition rates, Paes de Barros and Mendonça (1998) found that educational performance tends to be better in places where principals are elected by school officials, parents, and students over age 16; where schools have been granted financial autonomy; or where school councils have been established. To control for unobserved heterogeneity, the authors included a series of controls to try to capture any relevant omitted variables, which reduced the magnitude and significance of the aforementioned effects. The only outcome for which the results appeared robust to the introduction of additional controls was repetition rates. Including additional controls highlighted the fact that granting financial autonomy to schools was more significant than introducing school councils or electing principals. The authors concluded that their results showed these innovations had a generally positive but modest impact on educational performance broadly defined. As to which innovation is the most promising, the authors attached more significance to financial autonomy and much less significance to the election of principals.

It should be noted that all analyses were done at the state level. This probably masks important within-state variance in SBM practices and outcomes that might lead to different results. In addition, although the introduction of additional controls and fixed effects (where the panel nature of the data allowed it) is likely to have taken care of a substantial fraction of the unobserved heterogeneity, questions remain about whether these variables adequately covered the range of unobserved variables, particularly time-variant ones.

Also, Carnoy et al. (2008) found that participation in PDE improved passing rates for Brazilian students in grades 5–8 by almost 10 percent. PDE participation had no statistically discernable effect on student attendance or dropout rates.

### *El Salvador*

The SBM reform in El Salvador was initiated in 1991 under the name EDUCO. Its main objectives are to increase access to preschools and primary schools in poor communities, encourage community participation in education, enhance the quality of schooling, and improve school management and administration by placing the locus of decision making closer to parents and communities. As is the case with most SBM reforms, improving student achievement was not among the program's original objectives.

EDUCO schools are publicly funded and students receive free uniforms, registration, and basic school supplies in addition to free tuition and textbooks. In return, the parents of EDUCO students are expected to contribute meals, time, and occasionally their labor to improve schools (Edge 2000). Community Education Associations are the distinguishing feature of EDUCO schools. Each EDUCO school has one ACE with five community-elected members. ACEs receive funds directly from the Ministry of Education and are responsible for enacting and implementing ministry and community policies and for hiring, firing, and monitoring teachers (Sawada and Ragatz 2005).

Evaluations of EDUCO in El Salvador have found a steady increase in student enrollments that may be attributed directly to the program (di Gropello 2006). Student enrollments in EDUCO schools went from close to 8,500 students at the launch of the program in 1991 to more than 320,000 students in 2001. This represents 50 percent of rural enrollments and 37 percent of total enrollments in grades 1–9 (di Gropello 2006).

With respect to effects on student test scores, Jimenez and Sawada (1999) used a two-stage regression procedure to try to correct for selection bias (in other words, to correct for the fact that schools choosing to become autonomous may differ from other schools in some unobservable variables that can be correlated with the outcome of interest). Despite their efforts, they found no statistically discernible effects of attending an EDUCO school on either math or language student test scores among third-graders. It should be noted that EDUCO schools tend to be located in very poor, rural, and isolated communities. Therefore, it might be reasonable to expect to see lower test scores among EDUCO students because of their disadvantaged backgrounds. The fact that there were no statistically discernible differences between EDUCO and traditional schools may be a sign that EDUCO students actually are performing better than they would have in the absence of EDUCO.

In addition, after controlling for child, household, and school characteristics, Jimenez and Sawada (2003) found that EDUCO third-graders were more likely than third-graders in traditional schools still to be studying in that school 2 years later. Jimenez and Sawada's continuation probit coefficient for EDUCO schools was 0.36. This suggests that attending an EDUCO school raises the probability of continuing in school by 64 percent (translating the z-coefficient into probabilities using the normal distribution), compared with attending a non-EDUCO school.

These results attempt to control for selection bias, and they use 1996 test scores to control for initial differences in achievement that might affect dropout behaviors between traditional and EDUCO schools. The authors also found that supply-side constraints were important in EDUCO schools. The fact that most EDUCO schools do not offer grades 4–6 affects continuation rates. This is evident because, if the variable measuring the number of second-cycle sections in the schools is dropped from the models, the EDUCO dummy loses significance. To investigate the EDUCO effect further, the authors added a community participation variable to the estimation. The EDUCO coefficient lost magnitude and significance, and community participation emerged as a positive and statistically significant variable. The authors thus concluded that a significant portion of the EDUCO effect may be explained by community participation (Jimenez and Sawada 2003).

With respect to effects on teachers' behavior, Jimenez and Sawada (1999) found that students in EDUCO schools are less likely to miss school because of teacher absences. A more recent study by Sawada (2000) measured teacher effort in terms of their overall attendance and the number of hours they spend on parent-teacher meetings. He found that EDUCO teachers make more effort (only when effort is defined as hours of parent-teacher meetings) than do teachers in traditional schools. Sawada used instrumental variables to reduce the endogeneity between community participation and observed effort.

Sawada and Ragatz (2005) tried to improve the methodology that had been used by Jimenez and Sawada (1999) and Sawada (2000) by using propensity score matching to identify the EDUCO effect on teacher behavior, administrative processes, and, ultimately, student test scores. They found that community associations managing EDUCO schools felt that they had more influence in virtually every administrative process than did the equivalent associations in traditional schools. In particular, the hiring and firing of teachers appeared to be one of the administrative processes over which the EDUCO associations had the most influence. The authors also found that teachers in EDUCO schools spent more time meeting with parents and more time teaching, and they were absent fewer days than teachers in traditional schools. However, the effects of these factors on student test scores were not statistically significant. Nonetheless, these results lend support to the idea that devolving autonomy over decision making to the school level leads to a closer monitoring of teachers, which then results in greater teacher effort.

Last, with respect to parental involvement, Jimenez and Sawada (2003) found that parent associations in EDUCO schools visited classrooms more than once a week, on average—a number of visitations three to four times greater than that of parent associations in traditional schools. Sawada (2000) found that EDUCO schools had better classroom environments (measured by smaller class sizes and the availability of a classroom library), leading to higher student test scores in third grade.

### Guatemala

Initially piloted in the early 1990s in Guatemala, PRONADE was expanded in 1996 following the Peace Accords. The main objectives of PRONADE are to increase access to preschool and primary school for out-of-school children, decentralize educational decision making, increase community participation in education, and maintain indigenous and linguistic diversity (di Gropello 2006).

Under PRONADE, several key school administrative functions have been decentralized to community school councils, the COEDUCAs (Comités Educativos). These functions include paying staff salaries; hiring, firing, monitoring, and evaluating staff; setting the school schedule and calendar; building and maintaining school facilities; and providing budget oversight. The school council consists of 15 community members (di Gropello 2006). PRONADE schools are built in remote rural areas and provide preschool and primary education. To be eligible for PRONADE, communities must demonstrate they have the ability and interest to manage the new school, are not located near another public school, and have at least 20 preschool- and primary-school-age children.

When it began as a pilot program, PRONADE had schools in 19 communities in Guatemala. By 2004, there were PRONADE schools in more than 3,600 communities, with almost 400,000 children enrolled at the primary level. As of 2002, PRONADE schools represented 21 percent of primary school enrollments in rural areas and accounted for 14 percent of total primary enrollments in the country (MINEDUC [2004], cited by di Gropello [2006]).

With respect to student achievement, Marshall (2004) found that under some econometric specifications, attending a PRONADE school decreased Spanish and math achievement for girls (estimations were done separately by gender). However, he found that a PRONADE school increased the attendance of Mayan-speaking girls. In his study, Marshall used a 1999 sample of slightly more than 1,000 first-graders in 58 schools in three Guatemalan departments.[1] Additional data were collected for these children in 2002, including family background measures and test scores. Because this study was not designed explicitly to look at differences between PRONADE and traditional schools, it did not control for selection or other kinds of biases that may have affected these results. In addition, the data were not nationally representative.

A more recent study conducted by the World Bank (2004) used tests developed by the United Nations Educational, Scientific, and Cultural Organization's (UNESCO's) regional office in Latin America and the Caribbean. It found that controlling for student, teacher, and school factors eliminated any negative differences between PRONADE and traditional public schools, and even showed positive differences in the case of Spanish language studies (di Gropello 2006). However, this study does not appear to have corrected for selection or other potential biases.

There is some evidence that PRONADE increased community participation in Guatemala and that parental involvement (measured by parent-teacher meetings and director-parent meetings) was higher in PRONADE schools than in traditional schools (di Gropello 2006). Even though the school councils have the power to hire and fire teachers, fewer than 2 percent of them reported firing a teacher—a figure not significantly different from the number of firings in traditional schools (although this may have been because teachers in PRONADE schools are better).

Finally, researchers found teachers in PRONADE schools resigned at a much higher rate (three times higher) than did teachers in traditional schools. This may have been prompted by better salaries, working conditions, and job security in traditional schools (di Gropello 2005). In addition, CIEN (1999) and di Gropello found that PRONADE schools were more likely to lack water and sanitary facilities and that people generally thought PRONADE schools were worse-off than were traditional schools. In terms of teacher effort, one national evaluation found that PRONADE schools reported fewer teacher absences and more days worked during the school year (MINEDUC/DP Tecnología [2002] cited in di Gropello [2006]).

### Honduras

In 1999, Honduras implemented PROHECO to increase access to education and encourage community participation in educational decision making. In the 1990s, access was an important issue in Honduras. Some studies had revealed that more than 14 percent of school-age children (most of them living in rural areas) were not enrolled in school in 1997 (di Gropello 2006).

To be eligible for PROHECO, schools must be in rural areas, have at least 25 preschool- and primary-school-age children, and not be located near another school (di Gropello 2006). PROHECO schools must have a school council—a legal entity charged with overseeing the budget, selecting and paying teachers, monitoring teacher and student attendance and performance, and building and maintaining school facilities. The school council has six community members and it receives funds from PROHECO's coordinating unit, which receives those funds from the Ministry of Finance (di Gropello 2006).

The SBM reforms in Honduras have succeeded in increasing coverage in rural areas. In 2000, the program enrolled close to 40,000 students at the preschool and primary levels. In 2004, more than 87,000 students were enrolled at these levels, representing about 11 percent of the total enrollment in rural areas (di Gropello 2006).

Di Gropello and Marshall (2005) found that PROHECO schools had a modest but statistically significant effect in reducing student dropout rates. With respect to student test scores, PROHECO students appear to have higher test scores in science than do their peers in non-PROHECO schools. Selection bias appears to be underestimating these effects, so they should be taken as a lower bound. PROHECO seems to have had no statistically discernible effect on math or language scores. Because the data used for these analyses were weak, this evidence should be taken with precaution.[2]

A study of the impact of the SBM reform on teacher effort in Honduras (di Gropello and Marshall 2005) found that teacher effort was not significantly higher in PROHECO schools than in traditional schools. PROHECO teachers did not report spending any more time teaching Spanish or math than did teachers in traditional schools (the differences are not statistically significant), nor did they report working more hours per week. There is no evidence that PROHECO and traditional schools differ in their pedagogical methods (di Gropello 2006). However, PRO-HECO schools appear to have more resources and learning materials and better infrastructure than do traditional schools, and they report fewer closings resulting from work stoppages (di Gropello and Marshall 2005; di Gropello 2006).

Finally, parents of PROHECO students appear to meet less frequently with teachers and other school personnel than do parents of students in traditional schools. Both teachers and principals in PROHECO schools also report having less autonomy than those in traditional schools—a finding that is not surprising, given that the higher degree of autonomy enjoyed by parents at PROHECO schools appears to reduce the amount of autonomy felt by school personnel (di Gropello and Marshall 2005).

### *Mexico*

In 2001, Mexico implemented the Quality Schools Program to provide more autonomy to schools by giving them annual grants of up to of $5,000 to improve educational quality. In exchange for PEC grants, schools must prepare an educational improvement plan that outlines how they intend to use the grant. Parent associations must be involved in the design, implementation, and monitoring of the plan. In the first 4 years, about 80 percent of the grant must be spent on school materials and facilities. In the fifth year, only part of the money can be spent on such goods, and most of the grant goes to fund teacher training and development. Participation in PEC is voluntary, but the program targets disadvantaged urban schools. As of 2004, more than 20,000 schools, or 10 percent of all Mexican primary schools, received PEC support (Skoufias and Shapiro 2006).

Skoufias and Shapiro (2006) employed panel data regression analysis and propensity score matching to evaluate the impact of PEC on student dropout, failure, and repetition rates using a nationally representative panel data set covering the 2001/02 and 2003/04 school years. To establish a comparison group, they used student outcome data for fiscal years 2000 (the year before the first schools joined PEC) and fiscal 2003. Their difference-in-differences approach assumed no differences in time trends in student outcomes. To support this assumption, the authors included several controls at the school and municipal levels taken from 2000 data, such as teacher-student ratio, school type, and participation in poverty reduction programs. They also used propensity score modeling to match treatment with comparison schools based on these same data.

Skoufias and Shapiro (2006) found that participation in PEC decreases dropout rates by 0.24 points, failure rates by 0.24 points, and repetition rates by 0.31 points. To explore what brought about these results in PEC schools, the authors used qualitative data on PEC school effectiveness and parental involvement. They found that parents had increased their participation in the school and their supervision of students' homework. Moreover, students enrolled in PEC schools and their parents expected that these students would progress to more advanced education levels (Skoufias and Shapiro 2006). Unfortunately, the authors did not have qualitative data on non-PEC schools so were not able to investigate whether the changes that had occurred at PEC schools were unique and could reasonably be the cause of improvements in outcomes. Therefore, it cannot be concluded that these qualitative changes are attributable solely to the participation of the schools in the PEC program.

As opposed to Skoufias and Shapiro who used only 2 years of outcome data, Murnane, Willet, and Cardenas (2006) use longitudinal data from PEC's 7 full academic years. They found that PEC schools had a different outcome trend in the years prior to participating in the program than did non-PEC schools. To avoid violating this key assumption, Murnane and coauthors used the schools that entered PEC in its second year of operation (the second cohort of PEC schools, or "PEC2" schools) as the treatment schools. Unlike the schools that entered PEC in its first year, PEC2 schools had no pre-PEC outcome trends that were significantly different from the comparison schools and are thus a more credible counterfactual.

Their results show that participation in PEC decreased school dropout rates significantly (about 0.11 percentage points for each year of program participation). Given that the average dropout rate in their sample was 4.75 percent, 3 years of PEC would have reduced an average school's dropout rate by about 6.00 percent. The authors did not find that PEC had any significant effects on repetition rates. Last, they found that PEC had its greatest impact on states with medium levels of development, according to the Human Development Index, and its least impact on states with low levels of development. The authors hypothesized that this was because departments of education in these low-development states had less capacity to support PEC schools than was the case in more developed states (Murnane, Willet, and Cardenas 2006).

A more recent study by Shapiro and Skoufias (2006) found that PEC reduced failure and repetition rates by 0.05 and 0.09 percentage points, respectively. They also confirmed the finding of Murnane and his fellow authors (2006) that participating in PEC reduced school dropout rates by 0.11 percentage points. Furthermore, Shapiro and Skoufias (2006) found that the beneficial impact of PEC increases substantially in schools where the teaching staff has more schooling.

Another SBM reform undertaken in Mexico was the Support to School Management Program, which began in 1996. AGEs provides cash grants (from $500 to $700, depending on the school's size) to parent associations to spend on any educational activity they consider appropriate. In most instances, this spending is limited to improvements to school facilities. In 2005, more than 45 percent of primary schools in Mexico had a parent association (Gertler, Rubio-Codina, and Patrinos 2006).

In their study of the impact of AGEs on intrayear dropout, grade repetition, and grade failure in Mexico's rural primary schools, Gertler, Rubio-Codina, and Patrinos (2006) found that AGEs had a significant effect in reducing grade failure and repetition, but no significant effects on intrayear dropout rates. Their study was conducted between 1998 and 2001 on a sample of 6,038 rural nonindigenous primary schools, some participating in AGEs and some not. They used a difference-in-differences regression approach to evaluate the intervention's impact. They measured all outcomes at the end of the school year on the explicit assumption that AGEs needs to have been in operation for some time to be effective.

The authors use the phasing of schools into AGEs to generate sufficient variation in the treatment variable to achieve identification. Schools participating in AGEs prior to 2002 constituted the treatment group, and schools participating in AGEs from 2002 onward served as a comparison group. To test the validity of this comparison group, the authors compared preintervention trends in the outcome variables controlling for school and state fixed effects and a dummy variable measuring if the school is a potential AGEs school. This analysis did not reveal significant differences in preintervention trends for schools participating in AGEs in earlier and later years. Although the insignificant differences in preintervention trends should have alleviated any concerns about bias resulting from endogenous program placement, the authors used school fixed effects to address any potential bias arising from time-invariant sources. The authors also tested for biases arising from changes in the distribution of students in schools, but found no evidence for concern (Gertler, Rubio-Codina, and Patrinos 2006).

A more recent study of AGEs by Lopez-Calva and Espinosa (2006) yielded additional evidence to support the earlier studies. Lopez-Calva and Esipinosa found that participating in AGEs had a positive effect on student test scores in grades 4 through 6 (in primary school) for both Spanish and mathematics. The authors used a propensity score matching strategy to identify their results. The results are robust to controls for such relevant socioeconomic variables as participation in the conditional cash transfer program Oportunidades and teacher and school characteristics, as well as for alternative stratification strategies.

### Nicaragua

The school autonomy reform in Nicaragua was implemented in 1991 with the goals of increasing community participation in educational administration, obtaining financial resources for schools beyond government funding, and increasing efficiency in the use of human and financial resources (Parker 2005).

Autonomous schools must have a school council composed of the principal, teachers, parents, and students. Members are either elected or appointed by local authorities. Although all council members should be active participants, most councils tend to be led by the school principal (Parker 2005). The size of the council varies with the size of the school (King and Özler 1998). Councils can hire and fire the school principal, and they are involved in maintaining school facilities and ensuring academic quality.

Autonomous schools receive their funds directly from the Ministry of Education, based on the number of students (although there is a sliding scale by which smaller schools get more than larger schools get). As part of the original reform, autonomous schools could charge obligatory fees, but that was eliminated by legislation introduced in 2002 that explicitly abolished the right to charge fees. Many schools, however, continue to encourage voluntary donations (Parker 2005).

King and Özler (1998) studied the effects of school autonomy on student test scores in mathematics and Spanish. They used a matched comparison design based on selecting a sample of treatment schools (autonomous schools) and a comparison group of nonautonomous public schools and private schools. Their data included a panel of two matched school-household surveys conducted in 1995 and 1997 and student achievement tests from 1996. The sample, however, was not nationally representative and suffered from missing data and other problems. Autonomy was measured as de jure (whether a school had signed a contract with the Ministry of Education to become an autonomous school) or de facto (measuring the percentage of decisions made by the school council rather than by the central or local government). The authors found that de jure autonomy had no statistically significant effect on student achievement. However, they found that de facto autonomy had positive effects on student promotion and on student achievement in math and language in primary school and on language in secondary school.

A subsequent analysis looked at the effects on student achievement of two more refined measures of autonomy (King, Özler, and Rawlings 1999). The first variable measured the percentage of decisions made by the school council concerning pedagogical issues (such as class size, curriculum, and textbooks), and the second variable was the percentage of decisions related to teachers (hiring and firing, evaluation, supervision, training, and relations with the teachers' union). The study's findings about the influence of autonomy over pedagogical issues on student achievement were mixed. This is not surprising, given that the SBM reform had no significant effects on schools' decision making on pedagogical matters. However, it appears that having more autonomy over teacher-related issues does have a positive and significant effect on student achievement in primary school (both subjects) and secondary school (language only).

Using more recent (and nationally representative) data from 2002, Parker (2005) found that school autonomy had positive effects on third-grade mathematics test scores but negative effects on sixth-grade math scores. There were no significant results for Spanish language scores. None of the teacher or school variables seemed to be able to explain the positive differences between autonomous and nonautonomous schools (where they existed). These results are derived from a propensity score model that matches observations at the student level.[3]

Last, increasing schools' influence over teacher-related decision making is the area of the decentralization reform in Nicaragua that appears to have had the largest effect on student achievement (King, Özler, and Rawlings 1999).

## Initiatives in Africa

There are various SBM reforms under way in Africa.[4] Some of the earlier efforts were conceived under the umbrella of "whole school development," a package of reforms aimed at improving school management, in-service training, and monitoring and evaluation, among other things (Akyeampong 2004). The holistic approach to school improvement has been implemented, with some variations, in countries such as Ghana and South Africa. In Ghana, the core objective of the WSD project is to provide professional development (in-service training) to teachers to help them improve their teaching and their students' learning. The South African WSD initiative is focused on improving students' academic performance.

Other countries (including Ghana) are now implementing SBM reforms similar to those that have been adopted in Central America. Mozambique, for example, was an early mover in SBM reforms, and it now makes small grants to schools that participate in the SBM program (World Bank 2008c). These schools are managed by a school committee that is able to spend funds on basic classroom inputs and teaching materials. As part of the reform, participating schools have to publish student achievement data and a report of how the money is being spent.

In this section, we discuss some of the SBM reforms in Africa for which detailed program and evaluation information is available.

### Benin

Following democratic reforms in 1990, a decentralization reform was passed in Benin in 1999. However, primary school education continued to be characterized by low enrollments, poor learning outcomes, and high student-teacher ratios. In an attempt to tackle these problems, the Ministry of Primary and Secondary Education implemented an SBM program in 2006.

The reforms aimed to make schools more accountable to their local communities by training and empowering school committees and by using mass media to increase the amount of school-focused information that was available to the local community.[5] More specifically, the program sought to increase the decision-making power of school councils and newly elected municipal councils to increase parents' participation in schools and to encourage transparent financial management. School councils in Benin have seven members at the commune (municipality) level and 13 members at the school level. Membership at the school level comprises six representatives of the parents' association, the school principal, two representatives of community organizations, the village chief, and three teachers. The school council has control over the school's budget, personnel management, pedagogy, and fundraising.

The program includes the following components: (1) joint meetings of school personnel, the school council, and the local community; (2) financial awards to teachers nominated through secret ballot by members of the school council; and (3) training in financial procedures and oversight skills for school council members.

A randomized experiment is now under way to evaluate the program. A baseline survey was completed in June 2008, and two follow-up surveys are planned for 2009 and 2010. An analysis of the data collected so far suggests that the existence and effectiveness of PTAs is positively correlated with the academic performance of students, as measured by their test scores on a national examination. Data from a randomly administered reading fluency test suggest that attending kindergarten, having electricity at home, and having literate parents or guardians all are associated with higher test scores.

Two intervention designs will be tested in the experiment. The first treatment involves the creation of SBM committees at school and commune levels. These committees have a well-defined structure, mandate, and schedule of activities, and the members receive training in management skills. In the second treatment, in addition to the factors included in treatment 1, there is a weekly radio program that covers the activities of the committees, disseminates reports, and promotes public debate on education outcomes.

Thirty-six communes were selected to test the effects of this intervention, out of a total of 70 communes. For each of the 12 departments of Benin, 3 communes were chosen at random. One commune received treatment 1, one commune received treatment 2, and one commune was selected as a control group. Wantchékon (2008) has analyzed the mean values and standard errors of variables of school, student, and PTA characteristics. Based on observables, the author found no significant difference among the communes selected for treatment 1, treatment 2, and the control group. The variables used to measure impact were student learning outcomes, enrollment rates, grade attainment, teacher and student attendance, community satisfaction, and the participation and financial contribution of the local community.

### The Gambia

In The Gambia, most schools have PTAs. These associations often do not have a clear mandate with regard to school affairs, and they have no authority over the functioning and management of their schools. PTAs usually are led by one of the most influential people in the community, often the community chief, who remains in the position for decades.

At the school level, the principal used to be the only decision maker for all aspects of the school's operation. In 2008, however, an SBM initiative was introduced that would involve all stakeholders in a transparent management of the school, with the goal of improving school quality and student achievement.

As part of the new SBM program, SMCs are being established, and the members of the committees and the school staff will be trained in the skills needed to manage the school. SMCs receive a grant to support teaching and learning activities.[6] In addition, a newly designed PTA constitution is being adopted.

An evaluation of this initiative is under way to measure the impact of the SBM reforms (including the provision of school grants) on teacher activities and student learning. The evaluation is designed as a randomized experiment involving two interventions: (1) the adoption of a new SMC constitution, the SMC training, and the school grant (this treatment is being called WSD treatment); and (2) the grants to SMCs. The evaluation will take place in approximately 273 schools, out of which 90 were randomly selected for the WSD treatment, 94 for the grant only, and 89 chosen for the control group.

### Ghana

In 1995, Ghana enacted the Free Compulsory Universal Basic Education reforms. These reforms emphasized the importance of community participation in effective education delivery, and they mandated a review of education management structures at all levels to bring the administration of and responsibility for services closer to the community. Even before these reforms were implemented, the Ghana Education Service Act of 1994 created school management committees (SMCs), community-based institutions representing the entire community of a particular school or a cluster of schools. The purpose of the SMCs is to ensure that basic education students receive the best education possible. Committees are made up of 15 members, including the principal, PTA members, and other community representatives (World Bank 2008b).

As in Rwanda, the Ghanaian government gives capitation grants directly to schools on a per-student basis. SMCs may use these capitation grants to purchase school supplies and to hire additional teachers.

The World Bank will conduct an impact evaluation of the Ghana SBM program to test the effect of information and the creation of SMCs on financial and educational outcomes at the school level. In particular, the evaluation will test two interventions. The first intervention is designed to provide SMCs with specific guidelines and training to help them fulfill their role and give them information on the status of their school's performance and financial expenditures so as to increase accountability. The second intervention will provide treatment schools with relevant information only, no training. The evaluation will be randomized at the school level with 100 treatment and 100 control schools. Baseline data will be collected at the end of 2008.

### Kenya

In Kenya, community participation in schools happens through school committees. These committees or parent-teacher associations include elected parents and representatives from the District Education Board. In general, a committee's responsibilities are limited to suggesting promotions and transfers of teachers through the Ministry of Education, overseeing expenditures from capitation grants, and participating in the design and implementation of school development plans. Although historically most teachers in Kenya were hired centrally through the Ministry of Education, Science, and Technology's Teachers Service Commission, some school committees hired teachers locally, using financial contributions from parents. These teachers were called PTA teachers. New graduates of teacher training colleges often worked for several years as PTA teachers and then obtained positions as civil service teachers (Duflo, Dupas, and Kremer 2007).

With the introduction of free primary school in Kenya, parents no longer were required to pay fees. This resulted in large increases in student enrollment, but it meant that school committees no longer could raise sufficient funds to pay for PTA teachers, so pupil-teacher ratios increased significantly in Kenyan primary schools. A pilot project implemented between 2005 and 2007, with funding from the World Bank and International Child Support Africa (ICS), gave PTAs the funds to hire an extra teacher (Duflo, Dupas, and Kremer 2007).

The program, called the Extra Teacher Program, was designed as a randomized experiment, and it provided funds to 140 schools (randomly selected from a pool of 210 schools) to hire an extra teacher for first-grade classes. These teachers were hired locally, at perhaps a quarter of the cost of civil service teachers, but they had the same academic qualifications.[7] When a teacher had been hired, the ICS disbursed funds to the school committees. School committees then paid the extra teacher a monthly salary. When the program continued the following school year, school committees were free to replace or keep the extra teachers and were encouraged to move the teachers to second grade with the same group of students.

In half of these 140 schools (hereafter referred to as "nontracked" ETP schools), first-grade students were assigned randomly to either the contract teacher or a civil service teacher (in nontracked ETP schools). In the other half (hereafter referred to as the "tracked" ETP schools), first-grade classes were divided into two sections by initial achievement and then the sections were assigned randomly to either a contract teacher or a civil service teacher. In addition, among the 140 schools sampled to receive funding to hire a contract teacher locally, 70 schools were selected randomly to participate in an SBM intervention.

The SBM intervention was designed to empower the school committees to monitor teachers' performance. In each SBM-treatment school, the school committee held a formal review meeting at the end of the program's first school year (2005) to assess the contract teacher's performance and decide whether to renew his or her contract or to find a replacement. To prepare each school committee for this task, the ICS gave members a short, focused training course on how to monitor the contract teacher's performance. Committee members were taught techniques for soliciting input from parents and checking teacher attendance. A formal subcommittee comprising parents of first-graders was formed to evaluate the contract teacher and deliver a performance report at the end of the first year (Duflo, Dupas, and Kremer 2007).

Eighteen months into the program, students in all treatment schools had test scores that, on average, were 23 percent of a standard deviation higher than the scores of students assigned to civil service teachers. Also, the scores were 30 percent of a standard deviation higher than those of students in non-ETP schools. All differences were statistically significant at conventional levels. The effect of the contract teacher appeared to be larger when the school committee was given training in how to handle the contract teachers. The authors also reported evidence that the SBM initiative was helpful in raising the test scores of the students of civil service teachers, just as it was successful in decreasing the classroom absence rates of these teachers. Students with civil service teachers in ETP schools that participated in the SBM program scored 0.18–0.24 standard deviations higher in mathematics than did their counterparts in ETP schools not participating in the SBM program (Duflo, Dupas, and Kremer 2007).

A more detailed look at the results suggests that, with respect to teacher absences, civil service teachers in nontracked schools that did not participate in the SBM program were more likely to be absent from class than were teachers in the comparison group (teacher attendance fell by 21 percentage points). The authors argue that this finding suggests that civil service teachers took advantage of the presence of the extra contract teachers and worked less. However, civil service teachers in nontracked SBM schools were 7.8 percentage points more likely to be found in class teaching during random spot checks by the ICS. The authors argue that the SBM initiative likely emphasized the responsibility of the contract teachers with respect to the specific classes to which they were assigned and thus made it more difficult for the principal or the civil service teachers in those schools to use the extra teachers to relieve themselves of their own duties when they actually did show up at school. Also, the contract teachers in these schools had a greater incentive to please the school committee and less of an incentive to please the other teachers and the principal (Duflo, Dupas, and Kremer 2007).

In sum, Duflo and her colleagues concluded that simply introducing a new contract teacher and randomly assigning students to either this new teacher or the civil service teacher without training the school committee and without tracking by initial achievement had a small (13 percent of a standard deviation) but insignificant effect on test scores, despite class size being reduced by about 40 students. The effect is larger (19 percent of a standard deviation, significant at the 10 percent level) when the school committees are given training on how to manage the contract teachers (Duflo, Dupas, and Kremer 2007).

The researchers argue that the SBM initiative reinforced the role of parents (as opposed to that of principals who often dominate those committees) in hiring, monitoring, and retaining the contract teachers. Although parents were instructed on how to monitor the contract teachers, the SBM initiative did not have a significant impact on the attendance records of or the efforts made by contract teachers (perhaps because they already were satisfactory), but it did increase the efforts of civil service teachers. Furthermore, the authors assert that the superior performance of contract teachers might have been the result of school committees choosing better teachers or of the stronger incentives faced by contract teachers. Finally, the authors noted that contract teachers might have viewed their own good performance as a stepping-stone to a tenured civil service position.

## Madagascar

Since the 2002/03 school year, Madagascar has initiated several SBM programs. Many of these programs were launched as small pilot programs with the help of donors and eventually were scaled up nationwide.

There are three main types of SBM programs currently operating in the country: (1) school grants (*caisse école*), (2) community teachers (*enseignants* Associations of Parents of School Children [FRAM]), and (3) school councils (Associations of Teachers [FAF]). In addition, one other program that has been partially implemented in public primary schools since 2005 involves the development of school improvement plans (*contrat program*). This program, however, is not related to any school grant program.

The *caisse école* has been in effect since the 2002/03 school year. Since then, all public and private primary schools have received school grants to substitute for school fees that were levied previously. The allocation formula is per capita, with an adjustment based on the conditions of the school's location. The per capita amount for private schools is lower than for public primary schools. The objectives of the grants are to increase the schools' material endowments and improve the school environment. Schools may spend the money on teacher materials and school council materials, textbooks, sports materials, school maintenance and repairs, and any distribution and travel costs necessary to make these purchases. The school council manages the *caisse école* in each school.

The *enseignants* FRAM program is designed to support the hiring of community teachers. Parents' associations help raise the funds needed to pay for these teachers; and, since 2006, the government of Madagascar has subsidized their salaries. In addition, the parents' associations have a say in the hiring and firing of these community teachers.

The FAF serves as "a partnership for school development" among the various stakeholders at the local level. Its members are parents, the school principal, teachers, NGO members, local religious and business leaders, and local government officials. The FAF executive committee is elected for a period of 3 years. Finally, the *contrat programme*, implemented in 2005, is designed to help school management councils develop and implement annual school improvement plans.

An evaluation of the program is under way. It will consist of a randomized experiment with three different interventions aimed at understanding whether improved information flows among service providers and students have had any effects on student outcomes. The interventions will include training, school report cards, and management tools and guidelines. Some schools will receive all three interventions, whereas others will receive only one or two.

### Niger

In 2002, the education sector in Niger was decentralized and school management committees (Comité de Gestion de l'Etablissement Scolaire; COGES) were established. Grants were given directly to the COGES to increase the proportion of financial resources reaching the school level and to provide funding to execute the school action plans, according to local needs.

The COGES program includes two major components. First, school committee members receive training in the skills necessary to fulfill their management responsibilities. Second, schools receive grants that may be used to enhance their inputs, buy extra teaching hours, or improve their maintenance. These grants consist of a one-time lump-sum payment at the beginning of the school year (on average, $209 per school and $2 per student). The amount of the grant varies by the size of the school (that is, the number of classrooms). In 2002, COGES began to be established in public primary schools in three regions of Niger.

The school committee consists of a president, (a parents' association member), a treasurer (a mother's association representative), a secretary, the principal, and three members (one teacher's representative and two parent's association members). The committee may (1) decide how to use the school grant, (2) supervise and evaluate teachers, (3) consult with the school on the hiring of contract teachers, and (4) hire and fire community teachers.

An impact evaluation has been put in place to learn how the grants affect the functioning of the school committee, the management of the school, and, ultimately, the quality of the education being offered. The key outcomes to be measured are parental participation, school management (for example, teacher attendance and the development and implementation of the school improvement plan), repetition rates, and students' test scores. The evaluation is being implemented as a randomized experiment at the school level in two regions of Niger (Tahoua and Zinder)—regions where school committees already are functioning and the members have received training.

Three different interventions are being tested: (1) grants only, (2) grants plus financial monitoring of schools, and (3) grants plus a list of noneligible expenditures. Out of 1,000 schools, 500 make up the treatment group and 500 are left as a control group. To implement the evaluation, a baseline survey and student tests were conducted during the summer of 2008. The next follow-up is planned for the spring of 2009.

After the evaluation results are released, the government will consider whether to scale up the program nationwide.

### Rwanda

As part of a wider functional and fiscal decentralization reform begun in 2000, which gave local authorities the responsibility for service delivery and the power to raise revenue within their jurisdictions, the government of Rwanda has implemented various education reforms. These reforms were aimed at improving service delivery in the education sector by decentralizing budgetary and managerial decision authority. The main focus was on strengthening accountability mechanisms by encouraging greater district and community participation in the planning and management of school resources (World Bank 2008d).

Since 2005, the education sector in Rwanda has been decentralized. Schools at the basic education level are controlled by district education officers, school principals, and PTAs. Although PTAs have no authority over budgetary decisions or management of staff—that is, no power to hire and fire—they do have the power to reprimand permanent teachers and to be consulted in the hiring of contract teachers. Further decentralization of education decision making to the PTAs is a high priority for future education reform in Rwanda. The challenge, however, is to find ways to ensure full PTA participation in the school management process.

A major step in the process of decentralization has been implementing free primary education. School fees were abolished in 2003 and replaced by a capitation grant for all schools provided by the central government directly to schools on a per-student basis. The government deposits the capitation grants into school bank accounts. These school-managed grants substantially increased per-student funding for primary school students in the first three years of the policy (from $0.60 in 2004 to $10.00 in 2007). School councils can use capitation grants to purchase school supplies, give teachers bonus allowances (dependent on their successfully completing a set of requirements agreed between the teacher and the principal), and support the full costs (salary and bonus) of teachers hired on a fixed-term contract. School councils are made up of 10 members, including the principal and PTA members. However, anecdotal reports from Rwanda suggest that the principal makes most of the decisions with little input from PTA members.

The World Bank is designing an evaluation of the capitation grant SBM program in Rwanda. It will be a randomized school evaluation consisting of 100 treatment and 100 control schools. The aim of the evaluation will be to understand how the increased job security for teachers and the strengthening of school management councils have affected teacher performance, PTA involvement, and student test scores. The first part will evaluate the performance of contract teachers hired under the SBM reform. The second part will observe how school management committees have affected education decision making and whether it is possible to increase the contribution made by PTA members by providing them with training on school governance, management, or school functioning, among other topics. After being evaluated favorably, contract teachers in treatment schools will receive a permanent position at the school and will receive PTA training. Baseline test data for the evaluation will be collected in early 2009.

### Senegal

In Senegal, local education offices manage primary education and require schools to develop an annual school improvement plan or project. A new SBM initiative soon to be implemented in Senegal (Projet d'Ecole) will provide schools with financial resources (approximately $3,000 per school) to implement their plans. Under the Projet d'Ecole, a school committee consisting of teachers and parents must submit an application for these funds to a committee within the local education office, and that office will evaluate the different grant proposals according to guidelines provided by the Ministry of Education. These guidelines require that all applications focus on pedagogical activities (World Bank 2008e).

The main goal of the program is to improve school quality (as measured by students' academic achievement), specifically by providing more and better pedagogical resources in the school. Therefore, school committees will be able to use the grants to purchase pedagogical materials and inputs, as well as to fund teacher training.

A randomized evaluation of this project has started. Schools that have submitted eligible projects of sufficient quality and prepared by the committees will participate in a lottery that will distribute the available funding randomly. All schools are encouraged to apply for funding. Some of the applications that do not meet the minimum standards will be sent back to the schools so that they may revise and resubmit them for consideration.

The design of the school grants project impact evaluation includes two randomly selected treatment groups. The first group, which includes 100 schools, will join the program in 2008. Another 100 schools will be selected for a control group, but they will have to be excluded from the program for 2 years. The second group, which will include 100 more schools, will begin to participate in the intervention in 2009. It is uncertain whether the first treatment group will continue to receive financial support from the program during the second year.

If schools selected for the first period receive funding the following year, it will be possible for the evaluating team to test whether the extra year of exposure leads to further progress, relative to the control group. Moreover, if it is possible to collect data on a second cohort a year later and to follow the same children at the end of the second school year, it will be possible to compare the performance of children in the first cohort with that of the children in the second cohort (each against its respective control group). The evaluation will show whether the effects of the program become more pronounced the longer it operates in a school.

The baseline survey data were collected during the fall of 2008 on the following indicators—teachers' and students' attendance, availability of learning and teaching materials, teachers' activities and allocation of time, involvement of PTAs in school management, grade repetition rates, dropout rates, and test scores in math and reading/language. The evaluation instrument will include information about the school and about teachers and principals, and it will survey a sample of the students' households.

There will be two follow-up surveys. The first one will occur at the end of the 2008/09 school year and will collect data about the first cohort. If more schools are added to the program in 2009, data collected in the first survey also will serve as the baseline for the second treatment group. The second follow-up survey will be carried out in 2010, gathering information about all the children and schools that have participated in the SBM program during this period and information on those in the control group.

## Initiatives in Asia

In this section we present three cases of SBM in Asia: Cambodia; Hong Kong, China; and Indonesia. They vary in the amount of funds that the school receives, responsibilities of the community and PTAs, and scope of the instruments of decentralization.

### Cambodia

The EQIP school grants program began in Takeo Province in 1998 with a pilot group of 10 clusters, and it expanded to include roughly 1,000 schools in three provinces between 1998 and 2003. EQIP schools receive cash grants that are invested in priorities set by the local cluster committee—representing an average of six schools—as part of a cluster plan.

The grants program is designed to improve school quality in two ways. The first intended improvement is simply a resource effect because school clusters receive money that may be used to purchase additional inputs, like new equipment, teacher training, and student libraries. The second quality improvement is an increase in school management capacity produced by cluster schools gaining valuable experience in participative planning and in executing school plans. With decentralized planning and execution, the grants program is expected to result in a more efficient use of funds than standard, top-down educational interventions produce.

Qualitative reviews of the program so far have been positive (Geeves et al. 2002). The EQIP project has delivered the money in a timely fashion, and donors generally are satisfied with how the money has been spent. With respect to program evaluations, preliminary results from Benveniste and Marshall (2004) found systematic variation in spending by school clusters associated with specific school characteristics and parental participation. Nonetheless, the largest variation is associated with the year and province variables, suggesting that central forces exert considerable influence on local choices.

With regard to outcomes, preliminary results suggest that participation in EQIP is associated with marginally lower dropout rates, higher pass rates, and better academic achievement. These results are robust to the inclusion of controls for school and community characteristics and province-level fixed effects. For this analysis, the authors used regression analysis with 5 years of data and took advantage of the phase-in strategy to decrease the potential for selection bias. The empirical strategy was to regress student test scores on student, teacher, and school characteristics, plus controls for province and year. All community, school, director, and teacher characteristics were set at their 1998 pre-EQIP levels (Benveniste and Marshall 2004).

Cost-effectiveness comparisons generally are favorable, as EQIP money spent on specific activities—such as teacher development and infrastructure improvements—has been associated with higher returns than other possible interventions would have produced.

### Hong Kong, China

In 1991, Hong Kong, China began implementing a series of SBM reforms mirroring efforts in Australia, the United Kingdom, and the United States (Dimmock and Walker 1998b; Wong 2003). The School Management

Initiative (SMI) aimed to increase school effectiveness by establishing new roles for and relationships among the education department, school management committees, sponsors, supervisors, principals, teachers, and parents. Moreover, it sought to provide greater flexibility in school finance, increase accountability, and encourage collaborative decision making (Dimmock and Walker 1998b). In 1997, the Hong Kong, China, Education Commission broadened the scope of the reform and gave the SMCs autonomy over personnel decisions, financial matters, and the design and delivery of the curriculum (Wong 2003). Schools may opt into the SMI voluntarily and, by 1997, about 30 percent of all Hong Kong, China schools had opted into the system (Dimmock and Walker 1998b).

Early evaluations of the effects of SMI strategies in Hong Kong, China concluded that parental involvement was minimal after the reforms had been implemented (Dimmock and Walker 1998b). With respect to teacher and principal behavior following the SBM reforms, researchers found that the SMI reforms encouraged a school culture in which teachers and principals felt professionally empowered and motivated. However, they also concluded that there was no evidence that the SMI reforms actually had permeated into the classroom and were affecting the work of teachers and students (Dimmock and Walker 1998b).

### Indonesia

Over the last decade, the government of Indonesia has introduced elements of SBM into its education system by involving school personnel (principals, teachers, and other staff) and parents in the management of schools to make the schools more accountable and responsive to parents and students (World Bank 2008a).

However, it was not until the introduction of the School Operational Assistance Program (Bantuan Operasional Sekolah [BOS]) in 2005 that school committees had any discretionary money to exercise their mandated role. Based on the BOS experience, the government has taken another step toward cementing SBM and parental involvement with a regulation (Regulation No. 19/2007) that enhances the role of school committees.

Successful examples of community involvement in Indonesian projects—such as the National Program for Community Empowerment, the Urban Poverty Program, and the Kecamatan Development Program—all indicate that social pressure from an informed local community can help reduce corruption and the misuse of funds. The design of the BOS program already closely parallels the institutional and implementation arrangements pioneered by these community-driven development programs. A modified version of the program, School Operational Assistance Knowledge Improvement for Transparency and Accountability, will expand and build on earlier lessons, enhancing the role of parents and the local community in planning and approving school budgets for BOS funds and monitoring BOS expenditures.

The BOS program disburses block grants to all schools throughout Indonesia, based on a per-student formula. It is Indonesia's most significant policy reform in education financing in two important aspects: (1) the per-pupil block grants provide incentives for principals and teachers to focus on maintaining and increasing enrollment, and (2) funds directly channeled to the schools empower school managers by enabling them to choose how best to allocate the BOS grants. School committees, first introduced in 1998 under the Scholarship and Grants Program and the School Improvement Grants Program, were tasked with assisting in the selection of scholarship students and overseeing school spending on grants. School committees comprise representatives of parents, community leaders, education professionals, the private sector, education associations, teachers, NGOs, and village officials. They must have a minimum of nine members, and the chairperson must come from outside the school. All public and private elementary and junior high schools in Indonesia are eligible to apply for BOS funding.

By international standards, the Indonesian BOS program is a limited form of SBM, particularly compared with programs in Latin America. School committees have control only over nonsalary operational expenditures. The Indonesian SBM under the BOS program does not permit committees to hire or fire teachers or even to have any control over capital expenditures.

A comparison of pre-BOS data from 94 schools in 16 districts participating in the first Governance and Decentralization Survey module indicates that as much as one-third of the allocated resources may have failed to reach schools. The BOS program uses a very simple and transparent formula and provides mechanisms for scrutiny both from the top through the internal audit and from the bottom through community mobilization and oversight. Under the BOS program, where schools receive operational funds directly and the funds are allocated independently, opportunities for further SBM are created.

Using data from various household surveys and the Ministry of Education's information system, a 2008 technical assessment carried out by World Bank staff identified a number of positive developments to which the BOS program has contributed during its first years of operation. Most notably, the BOS program has made a significant contribution in reducing school fees (by almost 40 percent in both primary and secondary schools), increasing operational budgets for schools, and reducing leaks in the funds transferred to education. In addition, it has increased enrollment rates and reduced dropout rates. The decline in fees for poor students appears to have contributed at least partly to the higher enrollments and lower dropout rates that can be observed when comparing pre-BOS and post-BOS data. Furthermore, focus group discussions have shown that the BOS program seems to encourage parents to support their children's transition from primary to secondary school.

Last, the BOS program has been important for promoting and facilitating SBM and parental and local community involvement. In a World Bank Governance and Decentralization Survey of 1,250 schools, 68 percent reported that they had implemented SBM principles. Of these schools, 95 percent claimed to have experienced positive benefits. Most schools had seen improvements in their students' grades (66 percent of the schools surveyed), their attendance (29 percent of the schools surveyed), and discipline (43 percent of the schools surveyed). These results, however, must be taken with caution because they are not based on standardized tests or other measures nor on a rigorous (or even semirigorous) evaluation strategy.

## Initiatives in the Middle East and North Africa

Two cases are presented in this section, Israel and Qatar. These cases show a high level of heterogeneity, as is true in the cases previously presented.

### Israel

In 1992, in an effort to improve educational quality, the Israeli Ministry of Education commissioned a committee to explore introducing SBM in schools. In 1997, the municipality of Jerusalem was the first to introduce SBM into 60 of the 74 schools in the city (Nir 2002). Introduction was gradual, over a period of 4 years.

As part of the Israeli SBM reform, schools are expected to develop well-defined goals and a clear work plan and to implement extensive monitoring and assessment methods. In return, they are able to manage the part of their budgets that is not controlled by the central government and they have responsibility for personnel matters and for establishing a school council (Nir 2002).

Nir, using data from a 3-year study of teachers in 28 elementary schools in Jerusalem, found that they perceived the SBM reforms to be both opportunity and burden. On one hand, teachers expressed increased commitment to maximizing their students' achievement and greater expectations of professional freedom for themselves. On the other hand, teachers felt that their autonomy was unchanged and their commitment to the school (measured by their acceptance of the school's goals and mission and a willingness to exert considerable effort on behalf of their school) and to the social integration of children actually had decreased.

Nir used baseline information for the various indicators from 1998, the year prior to the actual implementation of SBM in those 28 elementary schools, to compare teachers' beliefs and perceptions between the two points in time. The author controlled for teachers' backgrounds and other variables that might have affected the results, but was not able to include a comparison group of teachers in non-SBM schools—a comparison that might have led to more conclusive findings (Nir 2002).

An earlier study of Israeli schools in 1998 (Gaziel 1998) found that principals in autonomous schools felt more empowered to make decisions relating to curriculum and evaluation, staff development, and school policy than did principals in centralized schools. Teachers in autonomous schools also reported a greater sense of self-efficacy, commitment, community orientation, and achievement orientation than did their counterparts in centralized schools. This study used data from a random sample of 41 public primary schools in the Tel Aviv district. Nineteen of the schools were operating under the SBM approach, and 22 were operating on the traditional centralized model. The principals of all schools in the sample were asked to complete the Principal's Perceived School Autonomy questionnaire. Teachers chosen at random were asked to complete a teacher survey. The study made no attempt to control for the potentially self-selected nature of the autonomous schools, which might bias the answers given by their personnel.

## Qatar

In 2001, the leaders of Qatar hired the RAND Corporation to design a reform of the country's education system. Beginning in 2003, a new system of independent schools was put in place, with the central government providing funding but having no say in the day-to-day management of the schools. The independent school model represented a move to a more decentralized system of schooling than had existed previously in Qatar. The basic aims of the reform were to widen the range of schooling options available to parents (with different missions, curricula, pedagogy, and resource allocation models); to reduce dramatically the degree of control exercised over schools by the central government; to increase the monitoring and evaluation of students, administrators, and schools; and to hold schools accountable for quality.

There was a positive response from potential school operators to the call to open their own schools. The Education Institute, the body that oversees and supports independent schools, selected operators for the first generation of schools (the 12 independent schools that opened in the fall of 2004) from a pool of 160 initial applicants. All 12 opened under 3-year renewable contracts. In 2005, 21 additional independent schools opened as generation II, and 13 more opened in 2006 as generation III (Brewer et al. 2007). RAND currently is planning to do an impact evaluation of the Qatar reform.

The reform was designed to allow many different stakeholders to become actively engaged in the school system. Operators may be groups of educators or parents, private education management organizations, private schools, or any other entity capable of providing educational and financial guarantees of its ability to attract a sufficient number of students and educate them successfully. The rules under which independent schools operate are referred to as "contract guidelines," akin to the rules of any contract that lays out each party's obligations. Students who had been eligible for government funding under the previous system continue to be eligible in the new, independent school system; and the government now pays the costs of their education directly to the school operators.

## Initiatives in Other Countries

SBM also has existed in Australia, Canada, and New Zealand for more than 25 years. Throughout the 1980s and 1990s, the British government increasingly devolved authority and autonomy to parents and teachers. The most important of these reforms was the 1988 Education Reform Act, which gave rise to two categories of schools: locally managed and grant-maintained schools. In both of these models, school governing bodies have more authority and autonomy over budget and day-to-day operations than they had before. Both categories of schools also have the power to hire and fire all teaching and nonteaching staff. Unfortunately, there are no rigorous evaluations of the Australian, Canadian, New Zealand, or UK programs so there is no convincing evidence of the effects of these reforms on student achievement.

Various forms of SBM have been implemented in the United States over the last 30 years, including programs in Florida; Chicago, Illinois; New York; and Virginia. In 1988, after years of deteriorating educational outcomes, public dissatisfaction with the school system and the label "worst school district in America," the Chicago School Reform Act was enacted (Shipps, Kahne, and Smylie 1999). The reform's central proposal called for SBM to be adopted in all schools, shifting authority from the state to local school councils (Drury and Levin 1994). Each school council consisted of 11 members—6 parents, 2 community representatives, 2 teachers, and the principal; in high schools, a student representative was part of the council. Parents and community representatives were elected every 2 years by a vote of parents and local residents (Hess 1999). Councils have the authority to hire the principal and all full-time staff (including teachers), and to establish the curriculum and methods of instruction (within the constraints of the Illinois State curriculum framework). Contrary to what is the case in most SBM reforms around the world, student achievement was an explicit objective in Chicago.[8]

Hess (1999) has argued that, after initial slippage, student achievement improved in Chicago public schools in the decade following the reform implementation. The author cites the fact that 94 percent of elementary schools had higher percentages of students above the national norms in 1998 than they had at that level in 1990. The gains for the majority of elementary schools had been substantial (between 4 and 8 percentage points). At the high school level, the results were less encouraging, although there seem to have been important improvements in math (but not in reading). In a study of 14 elementary and high schools in Chicago between 1989 and 1995, Hess (1996) found that student achievement improved in 5 of the schools; in 3, there were no major changes; and student achievement declined in 6. Three of the declining schools were high schools. These findings must be taken with caution because they are based on a comparison of mean achievement at two points in time, without the use of any empirical method to ensure that some or all of this increase actually resulted from the reform. In addition, there is some evidence to suggest that merely comparing average test scores of students above national norms is not appropriate because the test forms change from year to year and because there is significant school-to-school variability in student mobility (Bryk et al. 1998).

To address these concerns, Bryk et al. used data on one particular test that was used in Chicago during 1993 and 1995 and then was repeated in 1994 and 1996 with the same cohorts of students (for example, second-graders were given the test form in 1993, and then were given the same test form in 1994 as third-graders). This makes the gains in 1994 and 1996 directly comparable because they are based on the same pairs of test forms and levels. An analysis of test gains reveals that, for elementary grades 3 to 8, the 1996 learning gains were substantially greater than the gains in 1994 for both reading and mathematics. These gains represent improvements ranging from 10 percent to 40 percent over the 1994 levels, and they appear to be part of a longer-term upward trend in test scores—not merely one-off gains (Bryk et al. 1998).[9]

SBM reforms of various kinds also were implemented during the late 1980s and 1990s in the Netherlands and in Spain. The Dutch reform has one feature that distinguishes it from SBM reforms in other countries: empowering the principal—rather than teachers, parents, or the larger community—is one of its main objectives. Shared decision making within schools is not a goal of the reform in the Netherlands.

## Notes

1. In Guatemala, provinces or states are called "departments."

2. The bulk of the PROHECO evidence, particularly that relating to its effects on teacher effort and student outcomes, is based on somewhat flawed data. As di Gropello and Marshall (2005) describe, the data originally collected to evaluate PROHECO (in 2003) did not produce an adequate group of comparison schools. The authors thus collected additional data for 2002, but the comparability of PROHECO schools in 2003 with the 2002 schools is limited. The authors also raised serious concerns about measurement error in some key variables (such as parental involvement) and about the small samples for some analyses. Although they tried to do so, the authors were not always able to successfully use more rigorous techniques, such as instrumental variable estimation or propensity score matching, because of data limitations. All of these challenges reduce the strength of the evidence on the effects of the PROHECO program.

3. Another study by Arcia, Porta Pallais, and Laguna (2004) purported to have found that the SBM reform in Nicaragua had a positive effect on student achievement. However, their methodology was limited to mean test comparisons and tests for the significance of mean test scores and differences in test scores for centralized (traditional) and autonomous schools. Because that method does not include any student, teacher, or school controls that also might explain some of the differences, we do not report those results here.

4. This section is based on the work produced by the Africa Impact Evaluation Initiative at the World Bank, under the guidance of Arianna Legovini and with the collaboration of Muna Meky and Nandini Krishnan.

5. Reinnika and Svensson (2004) found that a newspaper campaign in Uganda that published the funding entitlements of each school and provided information on local officials' handling of a large education grant program was successful in reducing the misappropriation of school funds. This wide dissemination of information also had a positive effect on enrollment and student learning.

6. The grant amounts are $650, $750, $1,100, or $1,300, depending on the school's size and its hardship status, as defined by the Department of State for Basic and Secondary Education.

7. The monthly allowance in this program totaled K Sh 2,500 (approximately $35), putting it at the top of the range of what typically is paid to extra teachers by school committees in Kenya (Duflo, Dupas, and Kremer 2007).

8. To allow for measures of achievement, the city established performance standards for each school, based on the percentage of students being tested who were performing at or above the national norm on the Iowa Test of Basic Skills or its high school counterpart, the Test of Achievement and Proficiency.

9. It should be noted that, unlike other SBM reforms, the Chicago reform received substantial contributions from foundations and local donors. In 1995, the Annenberg Foundation awarded the city a 5-year grant of $49.2 million to improve public schools, and those funds were increased by an additional $100 million from local donors (Lee et al. 1999). On one hand, it could be argued that existing research is unable to disentangle the effects of these considerable resources from the effects of the autonomy reforms. On the other hand, evidence such as that of Bryk et al. (1998) compares gains in 1994 and 1996. Although the authors do conclude that gains were much larger in 1996 (after the Annenberg donation), it is unlikely that those funds would have had such an immediate impact on achievement.

# CHAPTER 3

# Evaluating School-Based Management Initiatives

This chapter reviews some of the features of rigorous evaluations that allow researchers to assess the impact of SBM programs. In general terms, an effective evaluation should include three important steps (Gertler, Patrinos, and Rubio-Codina 2007):

1. *Clearly define the intervention*—All interventions modify margins and incentives differently for different stakeholders. It is critical to define what is being modified in the program, the new set of incentives, and to whom the modifications apply.
2. *Describe how the intervention is expected to achieve the final desired outcomes*—Understanding how the intervention will lead to the desired result is fundamental for the evaluation. In general terms, sound economic theory should guide the analysis of how the intervention will affect the desired outcomes.
3. *Define the identification strategy*—This strategy is the mechanism by which causal effects can be attributed between an intervention (such as an SBM program) and a set of outcome variables (such as dropout rates or standardized test scores). To be able to attribute changes in outcome variables to the program, it is necessary to overcome the problems of self-selection.

Those three steps that are essential to the process of performing a rigorous impact evaluation are particularly challenging in the case of SBM programs. Defining the intervention is very difficult because of the complexity of the SBM concept. Likewise, how the intervention is likely to achieve the desired results will depend on the complexity of the specific intervention. Finally, it is difficult to identify causal effects because of the three sources of bias—the selection of schools by authorities in which the program is implemented, school self-selection into the program, and the process by which students are enrolled in the SBM schools. In this chapter, we discuss each of these challenges for the case of SBM.

## How to Implement Impact Evaluations

Based on our review of SBM impact studies, it is clear that retrospective evaluations (or evaluations based on programs already implemented and having limited data) are extremely difficult to perform. For example, it is very hard to find a valid instrumental variable (IV) that accounts for the problem of self-selection. It is preferable to carry out prospective evaluations on programs that have yet to be implemented so that baseline (preintervention) data may be collected in advance.

There are three main strategies that use randomization for identifying the causal effects of SBM programs: (1) strategies in which a randomization of treatment is implemented, (2) strategies in which the entry order into the program is randomized, and (3) strategies that encourage participation in SBM programs.

Randomization at the school level is quite difficult to observe in reality, so randomization at the geographic level is a feasible option. However, even if randomization at the geographic level is possible, reallocating students between schools will result in problems of selection. For that reason, it is critical to collect information on students who switch schools, and to analyze differences in the characteristics of students who stay in one type of a school and those who decide to attend a different type of school.

When randomizing is performed at some higher geographic level than the school level, it is important to have detailed baseline information. For example, using randomization when the units of observation are states can result in imbalances between the treatment and control groups because of the likelihood that there are not very many states to yield observations and because these states may have very distinct characteristics. Baseline data

**Box 3.1**

## 800 Models, 29 Evaluations, 8 Years to See Results

In a meta-analysis of the effectiveness of school-based management models in the United States (or comprehensive school reform [CSR]), Borman et al. (2002) reviews 232 studies with 1,111 independent observations. These studies represented 29 CSR programs in the United States. From these observations, the authors compute the size of the effect that these 29 models had on student achievement. They regress weighted effect size on the moderator variables to obtain the residuals from the regression and add the mean weighted effect size to each observation, thus calculating effect sizes that are adjusted statistically for all of the methodological variables. They find that the number of years of implementation of the CSR is a statistically significant predictor of the student achievement effect size.

**Effect Size by Years of Implementation**

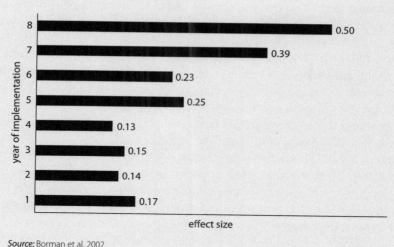

*Source:* Borman et al. 2002.

can indicate whether there are any differences (in observable characteristics) between the treatment and control groups, and then analysts can control for those differences in the estimation.

If pure randomization is not possible, then a strategy that randomizes entry time may be feasible. In this case, the order in which SBM is implemented in localities can be chosen by lottery. A simple example is the case in which the program is implemented first in one group of communities and then later in another group. The group that enters the program later is the control group for the initial participants. Ideally, the information would be collected at least three times—before the first intervention, before the intervention in the second group, and at some point in time after both groups have received the intervention. The last data collection point makes it possible to measure the intensity of the effects and the speed of the impact. Indeed, observing differences between the two groups enables analysts to make inferences about the speed of the program's effects because the first group will have been exposed to the program for longer than the group that entered later.

The last randomization strategy is to use an encouragement model. In short, active campaigns can be introduced to encourage a group of randomly chosen communities to participate in the program. These campaigns can include visits to communities by program promoters, NGO representatives, or social workers who explain the program and describe the potential benefits of the intervention. The rest of the communities will have access to general information about the program, but their participation will not be solicited actively. In this case, the promotion campaign is used as an IV of participation. Because the campaign is not correlated with the educational outcomes of the school in the community, but is correlated eventually with participation in the program, the instrument is a valid one. Hirano et al. (2000) and Duflo and Saez (2003) are examples of studies that have used this strategy.

In short, the ideal evaluation will use some form of randomization. However, if randomizing is not an option, RDD and difference-in-differences (DD) strategies are alternatives. First, an RDD procedure is suitable when the program is targeted using some continuous variable as the entry criterion. The estimation then will discover the true effect of the intervention (for example, the estimation is consistent) without the need for randomizing in the design of the program. This fact makes RDD a more flexible procedure than other types of techniques like propensity and matching estimators, especially for evaluating programs that already are in place.

The second promising nonrandomized strategy uses a nonrandom phase-in approach. It is possible to use this source of variation to evaluate the effects of an SBM program. For example, Gertler, Rubio-Codina, and Patrinos (2007) used this strategy. For this evaluation method to be technically sound, it is critical to ensure that the later treatment group has pretreatment observable characteristics similar to those of the group that enters the program first. This requires good preintervention data as well as good postintervention data.

## How to Define the Intervention

SBM programs take on different forms, depending on who has the power to make decisions and how much decision-making authority is devolved to the school level. Some programs transfer authority only to school principals or teachers; others encourage or mandate parental and community participation, often through school committees. Most SBM programs transfer authority over one or more activities: allocating the budget, hiring and firing teachers and other school staff, developing curriculum, procuring textbooks and other educational materials, improving infrastructure, and monitoring and evaluating teacher performance and student learning outcomes. Although we define SBM broadly to include community-based management and parental participation schemes, we do not explicitly include stand-alone or one-off school grants programs that are not meant to be permanent alterations in school management.

Based on this definition, the two key dimensions of the intervention are (1) to whom the power is transferred and (2) what types of decisions those people who receive the power are authorized to make. To define the intervention, it is important to identify both aspects. In terms of the first dimension, SBM policies may transfer power to parents, communities, schools, or a combination of all of them. Within a school, the transfer may be to the principal or head of the school, the teachers, and, in some cases, even the students. For example, the 1988 Chicago reform transferred power to both schools and communities, whereas reforms in El Salvador (1991) and Honduras (1999) transferred power to local communities alone. There also are cases where the transfer of power has not been as clear, making the evaluation of that program more difficult (for example, Nicaragua in 1991).[1]

On the second dimension—the type of decisions over which authority is devolved—the transfer of power may apply to a limited number or to a wider range of functions. An example of a limited transfer would be a policy giving the school or community a specific amount of money for any infrastructure improvements that it may deem to be necessary, as in the AGEs reform in Mexico (Gertler, Rubio-Codina, and Patrinos 2006). The transfer of power also may involve several different aspects of the educational process, such as decisions about the hiring and firing of personnel, the curriculum, the pedagogical method to be used, and the type of infrastructure investments needed. In Nicaragua, authority over almost all of the operational aspects of school management was devolved to the school level, ranging from the hiring of teachers to the maintenance of infrastructure (di Gropello 2006).

## Elements of Impact and Identification

How the intervention will produce the desired outcomes depends on which type of SBM program is adopted. The design of the intervention may be complex, involving several stakeholders and several inputs, or it can be a simple change in the allocation of a specific resource. The branch of the SBM literature written by education experts (for instance, Bauer, Bogotch, and Park [1998]) suggests that the impact of SBM programs can be measured by three elements—scope, decision making, and trust. Scope refers to the clarity of goals set by the members of the school council or the extent of the influence that the school has over input decisions. Decision-making practices are the school council's actual implementation practices. Trust refers to the interaction between the members of the community or council and parents.

This literature (for example, the original work of Bauer [1996, 1998] and of Bauer, Bogotch, and Park [1998]) has created several instruments to measure these three elements. However, the instruments and the scale of measurement are difficult to put into practice. For instance, several of the proposed measures are perceptions, which are subjective and difficult to compare. For that reason, this report suggests another course of action. Based on the economic theory behind SBM programs, we propose a different set of indicators by which to measure internal changes in the SBM schools. When inputs inside the school change, educational outcomes can change as well. Table 3.1 presents these two different kinds of indicators for measuring the outcomes of SBM programs in schools. The table presents four columns. The "dimension" column presents the key elements by which SBM interventions may change educational outcomes, such as information and accountability. The "objective" column discusses briefly the theory behind each dimension. (In the next section, we discuss dimensions and objectives in depth.) The last two columns of the table include the type of questions that the researcher may ask, and specific examples of question topics.

### Impact

The theory of SBM emphasizes that there are several ways in which this kind of intervention may change educational outcomes (Santibañez 2006; Gertler, Patrinos, and Rubio-Codina 2007). First, one of the main ideas behind SBM is that people at the local level (community members, parents, school staff, and students) have more information about the school than the central government has. This means that local people will make better, more appropriate choices for the school than will the centrally based

**Table 3.1  Inside the Black Box: How to Measure the Impact of School-Based Management Programs**

| Dimension | Objective | Type of question | Examples of questions/topics |
|---|---|---|---|
| *Education literature* | | | |
| Scope | Clarity of goals and the real influence of the board | Self-diagnosis; site team (for example, the community, council, or school board) | Site team members agree on what kinds of decisions the team may and may not make or the site team has real influence on issues of importance |
| Decision making | Actual implementation practices | Self-diagnosis; site team | Members work to implement decisions when they have been made or to correct problems that arise during the implementation of team decisions |
| Trust | Interaction between members | Self-diagnosis; site team | All members of the site team have an equal opportunity to be involved in decisions; site team members communicate openly and honestly during meetings |
| *Economic literature* | | | |
| Information at the local level | Changes in decisions | Key decisions about personnel (teachers and administrative staff) | Hiring, firing, rotation time, and teacher training, among others; who makes these decisions |
| | | Key decisions about spending | Spending on infrastructure and training of teachers |
| | | Changes in educational process | Change in pedagogical methods; changes in allocation of time; teacher absenteeism |
| | | Resource mobilization | Amount of resources from community invested in the school |
| Accountability and monitoring | Involvement of parents and community in the school and better accountability and monitoring | Direct involvement of parents and community in the school | Power of the board; type and number of meetings; decisions in meetings |
| | | Links between parental involvement and decisions at the school level | Do complaints about and praise of teachers translate into decisions about the teacher? |
| | | Changes in the accounting systems of the school | Implementation of an education management information system and changes in account tracking system |
| | | Changes in the attitudinal climate of the school | Changes in teachers' and students' attitudes about the school |

*Sources:* Education literature: Bauer, Bogotch, and Park (1998); economic literature: Gertler, Patrinos, and Rubio-Codina (2007).

Ministry of Education or even the local education authority. In this sense, it is important to track changes inside the school in the following areas:

1. *Key decisions about personnel (teachers and administrative staff), such as hiring, firing, rotation time, and teacher training*—It is important to know not only which aspects of these variables have been devolved to the school level and the frequency with which they are decided on, but also exactly who makes the decisions. For instance, is it the community or parents who have the real power to hire and fire teachers?

2. *Key decisions about spending*—It is important to track changes in the magnitude of spending on infrastructure, administration, and personnel training; and it is critical to determine who made those investment decisions.

3. *Changes in the educational process*—It is important to record any changes in pedagogical methods, such as how teachers conduct their classes and the extent to which students are encouraged to participate in the classroom (passive versus active exercises). SBM may change how teachers allocate their time among teaching, administrative tasks, and meetings with parents and community members. Also, SBM can change the rate of teacher absenteeism.

4. *Resource mobilization*—Greater community and parental involvement in school affairs sometimes leads to the school receiving more private donations and grants on top of the money it receives from the national government or from local taxes.

The second way in which SBM theoretically may change educational outcomes is in promoting more community and parental involvement in the school, and thus prompting closer monitoring of and more accountability by the people who are making decisions about school management. Along those lines, it is important to look into the following items:

1. *Direct involvement of parents and community in the school*—Ascertain what formal mechanism of interaction exists (for example, a school council) between community members and parents and the school, and identify who participates in it. Also, find out how many meetings have been held between the community and the school, and discover the types of meetings that have occurred (for example, meetings at which decisions were made or meetings convened simply for informational purposes).

2. *Links between parental involvement and decisions at the school level*—Discover if systematic complaints about or praise of a teacher by parents/community members ever translate into the firing or promotion of the teacher. Find out if parents' suggestions about infrastructure problems lead to expenditures being made to solve those problems.

3. *Changes in accounting*—By involving themselves in school affairs, community members and parents can persuade the school to improve its education management information system, its systems for tracking students' academic progress, and its systems for tracking financial inputs. In turn, these changes can improve the administration of the school and, eventually, its educational outcomes. For example, if having a better educational management information system liberates teachers from administrative tasks, then they will have more time to spend teaching.

4. *Changes in the school climate*—Community involvement can change the school climate either positively or negatively. It is important to gather information on the attitudes of teachers and students toward the school—for example, by asking direct questions about their level of satisfaction with the content of classes, among other issues.

Timing is one of the complexities that must be contended with in evaluating the impact of SBM programs. In general terms, such reforms take a long time to produce their expected outcomes. In the first year or so of an SBM reform, there is an adjustment period during which changes in personnel occur and management changes—such as creation of a school council—gradually are put into operation. In the short run, these adjustments may have a negative impact on educational outcomes, but once the school adjusts to the innovations, positive changes can be expected.

The speed of the effect depends as well on the type of outcomes being assessed. Some changes occur faster than others because the incentives that drive them are easier to effect. For instance, attendance rates, measured by the number of days when a student is present at school, may be easier and faster to change than are enrollment rates. So, in the short run, an SBM intervention may have a positive impact on attendance, reducing repetition, and failure rates, but such outcomes as dropout rates or test scores will take longer to improve.

In the United States, it has been argued that SBM needs about 5 years to bring about fundamental changes at the school level and about 8 years to yield changes in indicators that are difficult to modify—test scores, for example (Borman et al. 2003; Cook 2007). Box 3.1 synthesizes the evidence of 800 models and 29 evaluations to test this hypothesis, and it concludes that the projects started to deliver results after an average of 8 years. However, given the wide range of different designs that is possible for SBM programs, it is important to find robust evidence to back up this general assumption for each instance of SBM reform, especially in developing countries.

### Identification

As discussed in the introduction, identifying or isolating the impact of SBM programs is difficult because of program placement bias, self-selection bias, or sorting bias in how communities, schools, and students are selected to participate in the program. In the impact evaluation literature, a robust identification strategy is the randomization of treatment (Shadish, Cook, and Campbell 2002; Duflo, Glennerster, and Kremer 2006). In the absence of randomizing, however, it is possible to estimate the true impact of the interventions using other techniques, such as regression discontinuity analysis, IVs, Heckman correction procedures, DD estimators, and matching estimators. The first set of methods—regression discontinuity, IVs, and Heckman correction procedures—estimates the effects of a program either by using the entry rule to participate in the program or by modeling the program participation decision. The second set of methods—DD and matching estimators—constructs a comparable control group that has not participated in the program.

Randomization and regression discontinuity analysis both provide estimates of programs' true effects; in other words, their estimates are unbiased. In many cases, however, the design of the program does not allow for these types of analyses. In contrast, IVs, DD, and matching estimations (MEs) may be used when the policy design is not an experiment or when there are no definite cutoff criteria. The validity of these methods depends on some assumptions that, in some cases, are difficult to meet.

The following sections will discuss each of these techniques with reference to the empirical literature on SBM programs. Table 3.2 presents general descriptions of the most rigorous evaluations of SBM programs that have been conducted since 1995. The descriptions of several of these programs were discussed in chapter 2. The objective of this section is to present empirical evidence of the impact of SBM programs.

It is important to highlight two ideas before reviewing the empirical literature on SBM. First, only a very few rigorous studies of the impact of SBM exist. Santibañez (2006) presents a literature review of the 53 evaluations of SBM program impact on educational outcomes carried out

**Table 3.2  Evaluations and Impacts: Evidence of School-Based Management from the Most Rigorous Studies, 1995 Onward**

| Study | Country | Program | Duration of program | Data period | Estimation/ identification strategy | Limitations | Results |
|-------|---------|---------|---------------------|-------------|-------------------------------------|-------------|---------|
| *Randomization and RDD* | | | | | | | |
| Duflo, Dupas, and Kremer (2007) | Kenya | ETP | 2006–08 | 2005–08 | Randomized evaluation | External validity; pilot conditions might not be able to be duplicated in noncontrolled settings | Higher student test scores, lower teacher absenteeism, small changes in dropout rates |
| *IVs and Heckman correction models* | | | | | | | |
| di Gropello and Marshall (2005) | Honduras | PROHECO | 1999 | 2003 | Heckman correction model; exclusion restriction: presence of potable water and community services | Not a solid exclusion restriction | Small changes in dropout rates, no effects on test scores |
| Gunnarsson et al. (2004)[a] | Several countries | Several programs | Several years | 1997 | IVs: principal's attributes and legal structure | Not a solid instrument | No impact on test scores, positive impact on parental participation |
| Jimenez and Sawada (1999) | El Salvador | EDUCO | 1991 | 1996 | Heckman correction model; exclusion restriction: government prioritizing targeting formula | Not a solid exclusion restriction | Increased reading scores and decreased absenteeism |

*(continued)*

**Table 3.2  Evaluations and Impacts: Evidence of School-Based Management from the Most Rigorous Studies, 1995 Onward** *(Continued)*

| Study | Country | Program | Duration of program | Data period | Estimation/ identification strategy | Limitations | Results |
|---|---|---|---|---|---|---|---|
| Jimenez and Sawada (2003) | El Salvador | EDUCO | 1991 | Panel: 1996 and 2003 | Heckman correction model; exclusion restriction: government prioritizing targeting formula | Not a solid exclusion restriction | Increased probability of students staying in school |
| King, Orazem, and Gunnarsson (2003)[a] | Several countries | Several programs | Several years | Two points: 1995 and 1997 | IVs: principal's attributes and legal structure | Not a solid instrument | No effects on test scores |
| *DD and ME* | | | | | | | |
| Gertler, Rubio-Codina, and Patrinos (2006) | Mexico | AGEs | 1996 | Panel at school level: 1998–2002 | DD fixed effects; preintervention trends | Did not control for time-variant unobservable effects | Positive impact on failure and repetition rates, no effect on dropout rate |
| King and Özler (1998) | Nicaragua | ASP | 1991–93 | Pseudopanel; 1995 and 1997 | ME, panel data | No pretrend validation | De jure autonomy, no impact; real autonomy (hire and fire teachers), positive impact on standardized test scores |

| Study | Country | Program | Year | Year | Method | Limitation | Result |
|---|---|---|---|---|---|---|---|
| Lopez-Calva and Espinosa (2006) | Mexico | AGEs | 1996 | 2003–04 | ME, cross-section | No baseline data | Positive impact on test scores |
| Murnane, Willet, and Cardenas (2006) | Mexico | PEC | 2001 | Several sources: 2000–04 | DD; more systematic check of equal trends between treatment and control groups | Did not control for time-variant unobservable effects | Positive impact on dropout rates, no effect on repetition |
| Paes de Barros and Mendonça (1998) | Brazil | Decentralization | 1982 | Panel, state level: 1981–93 | DD; no preintervention trends | Aggregation of data; no pretrend validation | Positive impact on repetition and dropout rates, no impact on test scores |
| Parker (2005) | Nicaragua | ASP | 1991–93 | 2002 | ME, panel data | No pretrend validation | Positive impact on test scores |
| Sawada and Ragatz (2005) | El Salvador | EDUCO | 1991 | 1996 | ME, cross-section | No baseline data | Positive impact on test scores |
| Skoufias and Shapiro (2006) | Mexico | PEC | 2001 | 2000–03 | ME with DD; 1-year preintervention trend | No pretrend validation | Positive impact on dropout, failure, and repetition rates |

*Sources:* Cited articles; Santibáñez 2006.

*Note:* AGEs = Support to School Management program; ASP = Autonomous School Program; DD = difference-in-differences; EDUCO = Education with Community Participation; ETP = Extra Teacher Program; IV = instrumental variable; ME = matching estimation; PEC = Quality Schools Program; PROHECO = Community-Based Education Program; RDD = regression discontinuity design; SBM = school-based management.

a. School self-reported levels of autonomy.

since 1995. Additional research was conducted for this report, and it increased to 54 the number of evaluations reviewed.[2] This report deliberately discusses only those studies that made a clear attempt to correct problems of endogeneity, and that reduces the original number of 54 to a total of 14.

Second, despite the fact that, to our knowledge, these 14 studies are the best estimates available, some of them have serious limitations. For instance, five studies used IV approaches with questionable instruments. Four studies used ME, some of them with limited or no baseline information. Only two of the studies that used DD estimations verified the equality of trends between the control and treatment groups before the intervention. And one study (Duflo, Dupas, and Kremer 2007) reported an actual randomized evaluation of SBM efforts. Nevertheless, these 14 studies represent the best effort to date to estimate the effects of SBM, albeit with limited data.

It also is challenging to evaluate the size of the effects of SBM programs because of the heterogeneous presentation of metrics and results in the different studies. Several studies only reported the estimated coefficient of impact and, therefore, it is very difficult to translate these effects of SBM into a homogeneous metric because they depend on the specific measurement of both the independent and dependent variables. Others presented information on the percentage changes in some outcome variables as a result of the intervention. Again, the metric of the output variables differs considerably among studies. Nonetheless, we report the size of effects for those studies that have a clear interpretation of the results; otherwise, we indicate the direction and significance of the coefficient of impact.

***Randomization and RDD.*** Randomization and RDD produce unbiased estimators of the impact of SBM programs. Unfortunately, only one evaluation of the effects of SBM on educational outcomes using randomized evaluations has been done since 1995 (Duflo, Dupas, and Kremer 2007). However, several ongoing rigorous evaluations in countries like Indonesia, Kenya, Nepal, Pakistan, and Sri Lanka, among others, will increase our knowledge of SBM in the near future.

Randomization in impact evaluations is based on the idea that a lottery de facto will create treatment and control groups that are similar in terms of observable and unobservable characteristics. In this sense, the mean of observable variables and unobservable variables will be equal across groups. The only difference between the treatment and control groups is the intervention. Therefore, any differences in outcomes can be attributed solely to the program. For example, in a case in which randomization is used to assess changes in SBM schools, randomizing would be done at two levels. First, the schools that are to participate in the SBM program are picked by chance and then students are assigned randomly to the SBM schools. Any difference in educational outcomes, such as dropout rates, between the SBM and the other schools thus can be attributed to the intervention because there was no self-selection.

Usually in randomized experiments, data must be collected for a minimum of two points in time. Data on the treatment and control communities, schools, and students are collected before the intervention (baseline information), and then data on the same indicators are collected after the program has been implemented. The baseline data set is important because it can be used to test whether the randomization was implemented correctly and whether the two groups (treatment and control) are similar in (at least) their observable characteristics—in essence, the baseline validates the randomization. In the case of SBM, the outcome variables may be processes, like the ones described in table 1.1, or educational variables such as repetition rates, dropout rates, absentee rates, failure rates, and test scores.

The timing of the collection of follow-up data is critical in SBM reforms. Collecting these data too soon after the implementation of the reform probably will reflect only the adjustment period and may show the program's impact to be negative. After the adjustment period, however, SBM policies can be expected to start delivering positive results so it is important to allow a sufficiently long period of time to pass before collecting follow-up data. Also, it is advisable to collect more than one round of follow-up data.

One study that we reviewed reported the results of a randomized evaluation. This was the SBM element of the Extra Teacher Program in Kenya (Duflo, Dupas, and Kremer 2007). The intervention was implemented using a randomization design. One hundred forty schools were selected for the study. In half of them (the nontracked ETP schools), first-grade students randomly were assigned to either the contract teacher or a civil service teacher. In the other half (the tracked ETP schools), first-grade classes were divided by initial achievement into two sections and then randomly assigned either to a civil service teacher or to a contract teacher. In addition, among the 140 schools sampled to receive funding to hire a contract teacher locally, 70 schools were selected randomly to participate in an SBM intervention. As discussed previously, other SBM interventions in Africa and elsewhere have been implemented using similar randomized designs that would allow for causal interpretation of program results.

One of the difficulties in evaluating SBM programs is that they are often very complex interventions. Even if it is possible to randomize and, thus, attribute any difference in educational outcomes to the SBM program, it is not possible to attribute the impact to any specific change among the many changes that may have been brought about by the program. For example, an SBM program may change both how the decision to hire teachers is made and how teachers allocate their time. Even if, using a randomized experiment, we were to discover that the program had improved educational outcomes, it would be difficult to distinguish whether the improvements resulted from the change in hiring practices or the change in how the teachers spent their time. For this reason, it is crucial to analyze all internal changes in the school to understand which specific changes at the school level are affecting educational outcomes.

It also is possible to use RDD if the program identified its beneficiaries using an assignment variable. For example, in some states in Mexico, PEC uses a poverty index that is used also by the conditional cash transfer program Oportunidades (Skoufias and Shapiro 2006) to identify schools that qualify for the program's benefits. Other states rank schools by the quality of their improvement plans. Regression discontinuity analyses can be used in such cases because they make use of the assignment variable and the observations with scores close to the cutoff point to establish eligibility for the program. If all schools with a score below a certain cutoff are enrolled in the program and those with a score above the cutoff are denied access to the program, then schools with scores just below the cutoff point (beneficiaries) may be very similar to those schools that are just above the cutoff point (the comparison group). In this case, it is possible to compare the outcome variables for those two groups and attribute the differences to the effects of the program, given that we expect the schools in the two groups to have very similar characteristics. Regression discontinuity analysis resembles a randomization because, from the point of view of the school, to be "just below" or "just above" the arbitrary cutoff point is almost like taking part in a lottery. Unfortunately, to the best of our knowledge there is no SBM evaluation that uses an RDD design.

The difficulty with this approach, however, is the potentially limited number of observations around the cutoff point. Since RDD estimates the effects of the program using observations around the cutoff point, it requires a smooth assignment variable with a large number of observations on both sides of the cutoff value. If there are only a few observations, then the estimate of the impact will be very imprecise.

Furthermore, it is important to note that RDD is a local estimator; in other words, the estimation gives evidence of the program's impact on individuals close to the cutoff point but says nothing about its impact on those individuals with low (or high) scores. On one hand, this characteristic of RDD is a limitation because it is not possible to estimate the average effect of the program. On the other hand, this characteristic can be desirable because, in certain situations, the most relevant impact is that on the margin—the impact close to the cutoff point.

***IVs and Heckman correction models.*** Both IV estimation and Heckman correction models base their identification strategy on a variable that can explain the participation of communities and/or schools in the program (Heckman 1976; Angrist and Imbens 1995). The IV approach uses a variable with two characteristics—it can explain participation in the program but is uncorrelated with the outcome measures of interest. For example, the evaluator of a hypothetical training program that targets people born in a certain month of the year may want to determine the impact of the training program on the probability of its graduates becoming employed. In this case, given that the candidates' birth months are correlated with their entry into the program but presumably are not correlated with the probability of them being employed, the month of birth can be used as an IV.

The main problem with the IV approach is finding a valid instrument—in other words, a variable correlated with the decision to participate but not with the final outcome of interest. Most available variables correlated with participation are correlated with the outcome as well. Even if it is possible to find a variable correlated with participation, it is impossible to test whether the variable is uncorrelated with the unobservable part of the outcome variable.

Two studies used IV to estimate the effects of SBM. More precisely, these two analyses studied the effect that self-reported school autonomy has had on test scores. Gunnarsson et al. (2004) used 1997 regional test score data from several Latin American countries, and King, Orazem, and Gunnarsson (2003) complemented these data with 1995 results from an international standardized test, Trends in International Mathematics and Science Study. Both are cross-section, country-level estimations. The instrument that King, Orazem, and Gunnarsson used is the legal structure of the country (political stability, regulatory quality, and rule of law). This variable presumably is correlated with participation in the program. However, it is very feasible to argue that the variable is correlated with educational outcomes as well. As we described above, the instrument must not be correlated with the outcomes, so the estimation strategies used in these two studies present serious problems. In any case, neither study found that SBM reforms—or, more precisely, self-reported school autonomy—had any impact on test scores. According to Gunnarsson et al. (2004), scores in schools with the greatest autonomy are between 4 percent higher and 13 percent lower than scores in less autonomous schools.

The Heckman correction method is based on the estimation of two equations. First, it models the participation decision. For example, the dependent variable is an indicator of program participation as a function of variables likely to influence the decision to participate in the program. Second, it estimates the program's impact by regressing the outcome variable against the unexplained component of the participation equation—the residuals from the participation decision equation—and other variables (Heckman 1976).

In the Heckman correction model, there are two ways to identify the true impact of the program. The first method is to rely on assumptions about the distribution of the errors in the participation and outcome equations, but these assumptions are very unlikely to be valid. The second method is to use an "exclusion" variable—a variable that is in the participation equation but not in the impact equation—to estimate the impact. Clearly, this second method is very similar to finding an appropriate IV that can explain participation but not the final outcome and, thus, is as difficult to implement as an IV methodology.

Using the targeting formula as the identifying variable in a Heckman correction model, Jimenez and Sawada (1999) analyzed the case of EDUCO in El Salvador. The authors found that SBM had increased standardized test scores and reduced both student and teacher absenteeism. They also found that parents participated more in the EDUCO schools than in schools that were not in the program. Jimenez and Sawada (2003) used the same identification strategy but with panel data for 1996 and 1998. They found that SBM had a positive impact on the probability of students staying in school. As in the previous cases, the validity of the instruments used in these studies is questionable. In short, it is very likely that the program's targeting formula is correlated with educational outcomes, and that would invalidate the instrument used in both studies.

Using a two-stage procedure, di Gropello and Marshall (2005) evaluated the impact of Honduras's PROHECO. Their exclusion variables were community services and the presence of potable water. When they corrected for selection, they found that SBM had no effect on either teachers' efforts or test scores. Once more, it is difficult to argue that the IV was not correlated with the outcome variable.

In short, of the five studies using IV or Heckman procedures, only two showed that SBM had a positive impact on test scores, and only two found that it had a positive impact on dropout rates and on the probability of staying in school.

**DD and ME.** The richest evidence on SBM has come from studies using DD and ME. Some of the programs have extensive data sets that made it possible to use these two strategies to evaluate their impact. DD and ME methods generate a counterfactual using nonbeneficiaries who have characteristics similar to those of the beneficiaries. In DD, the true effects of a program are identified by verifying before the program starts the similarity of trends in observable characteristics between the treatment and control groups (Athey and Imbens 2006). In contrast, ME uses all of the observable baseline characteristics to find close matches in the control group for each treated observation (Rosenbaum and Rubin 1983; Heckman, Ichimura, and Todd 1998).

DD is more demanding than ME in terms of data. In DD it is necessary to have data for at least three moments in time—preintervention trends (that is, at least two data points before the intervention) and data capturing the changes that have occurred since the intervention was implemented. This amount of data rarely is available. Moreover, it is common to find studies that use data for only two moments in time, one observation before the intervention and one after for each participant. Results obtained in this way cannot be validated; in other words, it is impossible to say whether the estimated impact was caused by the program or was a trend that already existed between the two groups prior to program implementation.

Nonetheless, DD estimation has one important property: when estimated using fixed effects (for example, a dummy variable for each unit of observation and a dummy variable for each time period), DD controls for time-invariant unobservable and observable differences between the control and treatment groups. In other words, the fixed-effects estimation controls for differences between the two groups in both observable and unobservable characteristics that do not change over time.

Using ME in an impact evaluation requires rich and abundant baseline data. Furthermore, it demands that the process for selecting program participants be based only on observable characteristics. If some unobservable characteristic plays a role in the selection process, then the estimate will be biased. Moreover, because of data limitations, several impact evaluations using ME have been forced to use data to match the treatment group with a control group that was put together when program implementation already had begun. This procedure creates problems when the observable characteristics used for selecting program participants also change because of the intervention (Rosenbaum and Rubin 1983).

Evidence of the AGEs program's impact in Mexico is presented in Gertler, Rubio-Codina, and Patrinos (2006). The authors used the order in which schools entered the program to construct a DD estimator that controlled for fixed effects. They presented preintervention trends between the control and treatment groups, and found no differences in educational outcomes prior to the intervention—thereby validating the use of the DD strategy. They found that the program reduced repetition rates in 4.0 percent and failure rates in 4.2 percent of the treatment schools, but they did not find any impact on dropout rates. Lopez-Calva and Espinosa (2006), using data from 2003–04 and matching techniques, found that the AGEs program had a positive impact on test scores. The main limitation of their study was the lack of baseline data.

To estimate the effect of decentralization of school autonomy in Brazil, Paes de Barros and Mendonça (1998) constructed a panel data set at the state level between 1981 and 1993 (see also Carnoy et al. [2008]). They used a DD strategy with a fixed-effects model. The level of data aggregation (the states) meant they had to evaluate the program's impact with only a limited number of observations. In any case, they found that SBM had a positive impact on dropout rates (reductions of between 3.4 percent and 6.6 percent) and repetition rates (reductions of between 1.7 and 4.2 percent), but that it had no effect on test scores.

Two studies evaluated Mexico's PEC—a voluntary, urban-based program open to all public schools—using DD estimators. Murnane, Willet, and Cardenas (2006) and Skoufias and Shapiro (2006) used the same data source. Murnane and coauthors incorporated one more year of observations than did Skoufias and Shapiro. The latter authors used a matching DD estimation. The Murnane team argued that Skoufias and Shapiro's counterfactual had different preintervention trends, so Murnane and colleagues created another counterfactual using a new group of schools that had entered the program just then. Skoufias and

Shapiro found that SBM had reduced dropout and failure rates by 0.24 percentage points and repetition rates by 0.31 percentage points. In contrast, Murnane, Willet, and Cardenas found a positive effect only on dropout rates (an effect of 0.27 percentage points).

Evidence of the impact of the EDUCO program in El Salvador using ME is presented in Sawada and Ragatz (2005). One major limitation of this study is the lack of baseline data. The authors found that SBM increased the amount of time that teachers could spend on teaching, and that in turn translated into a positive impact on test scores.

In summary, six studies used DD and ME. Three of them presented evidence that SBM had a positive impact on test scores, and the majority of the studies presented evidence that SBM had a positive impact on reducing dropout, failure, and repetition rates.

## Notes

1. A general review of the Central American cases of SBM is presented in di Gropello (2006), and Bryk et al. (1998) describe the process in Chicago.

2. Many more papers and documents were read and included in this report. Among them are several World Bank documents (loan agreements, concept notes, and the like). However, none of them is included in this count because they are mainly descriptive reports of current SBM interventions under way around the world.

# CHAPTER 4

# Conclusions

The key argument in favor of decentralization is that it fosters demand at the local level and ensures that the kind of education that schools provide reflects local priorities and values. By giving voice and power to local stakeholders, decentralization can increase client satisfaction and improve educational outcomes. School autonomy and accountability may help solve some of the fundamental problems in education. If schools are given some autonomy over the use of their inputs, then they may be held accountable for using those inputs in an efficient manner. Decentralizing power to the school level also may improve service delivery to the poor by giving poor families a say in how local schools operate, and by giving schools an incentive to ensure that they deliver effective services to the poor and penalizing those who fail to do so.

SBM transfers authority from the central government to the school level, devolving responsibility for and decision-making authority over school operations to local agents—any combination of principals, teachers, parents, sometimes students, and other school community members. SBM-type reforms have been introduced in a range of economies, including Australia, Cambodia, Canada, El Salvador, Hong Kong, China, Israel, Kenya, Mexico, and the United States, over the last 30 years. SBM reforms in OECD countries share some common characteristics: increased school autonomy, greater responsiveness to local needs, and the overall objective of improving students' academic performance. Most countries whose students perform well in international student achievement tests give local authorities and schools substantial autonomy to decide the content of their curriculum and the allocation and management of their resources. An increasing number of developing countries are introducing SBM reforms aimed at empowering principals and teachers or at strengthening their professional motivation, thereby enhancing their sense of school ownership. Many of these reforms also have strengthened parental involvement, sometimes by means of school councils.

## Types of School-Based Management

There are many forms and types of SBM programs that vary as to who has the power to make decisions, how much decision-making power they have, and over what aspects of education they may exercise that authority. Four SBM models define who gets the decision-making power:

1. *administrative-control SBM*—in which the authority is devolved to the school principal
2. *professional-control SBM*—in which the main decision-making authority lies with the teachers
3. *community-control SBM*—in which parents have the major decision-making authority
4. *balanced-control SBM*—in which decision making is shared between parents and teachers.

Thus, in certain models the accountability of school principals is upward to the ministry, which holds them responsible for providing services to the clients, who in turn have put the policy makers in power and so have the ability to hold them accountable for their performance. In a number of SBM models, parents and the community have a say in decisions that directly affect the students in the school. In practice, SBM generally is a blend of the four models. The AGEs program in rural Mexico gives minimal autonomy to school councils, most of which are led by parents. At the other end of the spectrum, El Salvador and a few other Central American countries, as well as countries such as New Zealand, Niger, and Rwanda, have adopted a highly autonomous model, with most of the decision-making power given to parents. In the Netherlands and Qatar, parents may create their own publicly funded, privately run schools to meet their own specific cultural, religious, or academic needs.

SBM programs transfer authority over one or more activities, including

1. *budget allocation*—rare in developing countries, except in terms of authority over extra resources such as grants for school improvement plans
2. *hiring and firing of teachers and other school staff*—rare in developing countries, except in the case of several Central American countries following hurricanes or conflicts
3. *curriculum development*—very rare in developing countries
4. *textbook and other educational material procurement*—more common in developing countries
5. *infrastructure improvement*—very common in developing countries
6. *monitoring and evaluating of teacher performance and student learning outcomes*—usually part of school improvement plans, but rarely included even in SBM reforms.

The various combinations of the two dimensions of power devolution—to whom power is devolved and what powers are devolved—tend to make each SBM reform unique. In most cases, the recipient of the devolved authority at the school level is a formal legal entity, such as a school council or school management committee consisting of teachers and the principal. In nearly all versions of SBM, this school committee also includes representatives of the community who may or may not be parents of the children enrolled in the school.

## Autonomy and School-Based Management

SBM programs lie along a continuum in terms of the degree to which decision making is devolved to the local level, from limited autonomy at one end, to more ambitious programs that allow schools to hire and fire teachers, to programs that give schools control over substantial resources, to those that promote private and community management of schools, and finally to those that eventually may allow parents to create their own schools. There are both "weak" and "strong" versions of SBM, based on the degree of decision-making power that has been transferred to the school.

In moderate SBM reforms, schools have limited autonomy, usually over issues to do with instructional methods or planning for school improvement (Mexico's PEC is an example). The intermediate version of SBM is characterized by situations in which school councils serve in an advisory role (as happens, for example, in schools in Edmonton, Canada; in Senegal; and in Thailand). The strong form of SBM is characterized by councils that receive funds directly from the central or other relevant level of government and are responsible for hiring and firing teachers and principals and/or for setting curricula (as in El Salvador's EDUCO program). At the strong end of the continuum are education systems in which parents have complete choice and control over public education and where all decisions about schools' operational, financial, and educational management are left to school councils or school administrators (as, for example, in the Netherlands or in the charter school reforms in Qatar). The distinction between public and private schools at this end of the continuum is blurry.

## The Evidence Base

The number of rigorous studies of the impact of SBM is very limited. A few studies, rigorous and well documented, reliably measure the effect of SBM policies, but it is very difficult to standardize the sizes of the outcome variables because of differences in how they were measured in the various studies.

As discussed in chapter 3, the main findings from this limited number of empirical studies can be summarized as follows:

- Some studies found that SBM policies actually changed the dynamics of the school, either because parents got more involved or because teachers' actions changed. This was the case for El Salvador and Kenya.
- Several studies found that introducing SBM reduced grade repetition, grade failure, and school dropout rates. This was true in several countries, including Brazil, El Salvador, Honduras, and Mexico.
- The studies that had access to standardized test scores yielded mixed evidence. One of the studies showed strong positive evidence from a randomized experiment done in Kenya, where an SBM initiative implemented in randomly selected schools had large positive effects on student test scores. These effects were the result of a combination of smaller class sizes, more teacher incentives, and greater parental oversight. Positive effects on student test scores also were found in El Salvador, Mexico, and Nicaragua. Other studies reported that SBM had no impact on student test scores in Brazil and Honduras.

## On the Design of School-Based Management Programs

Despite the limited evidence base, we can offer a few specific ideas about the design of SBM projects, based on the large number of programs that presently exist around the world. Clearly, there are a few key issues that should be settled before policy makers undertake an SBM initiative.

1. *Specify what is meant by SBM.* The autonomy and accountability definitions must be explicit. The functions to be transferred must be delineated, and the entities to which they are to be transferred should be described. A clear account should be given of the resources that will be available, how they will be used, and what model will be developed (administrative, professional, community, balanced, or some combination).

2. *Take account of capacity issues.* In all models and types of SBM, capacity considerations are crucial. Thus, SBM projects should include a component to build the managerial capacity of parents, teachers, and other key players.

3. *Clearly state what is to be achieved, as well as how and in what time frame.* A good rule of thumb is that SBM reforms need about 5 years before any fundamental changes occur at the school level, and only after 8 years of operation can changes be seen in such indicators as student test scores. This has been the experience in the United States. Therefore, it is important to ensure that everyone involved understands the amount of time required so that their expectations are realistic.

4. *Establish goals, including short-term process goals, intermediate output goals, and longer-term outcome goals.* Most important, the relevant indicators must be measured before, during, and after the reform's experimental stage to make it possible to evaluate the impact of the reform. The high standards that usually apply to SBM programs in developed countries will be difficult to meet in developing countries. Even in developed countries, however, SBM reforms tend to take several years to produce any substantial impact, depending on the country's institutional context.

5. *Spell out what will have to happen at different stages for the reform to reach its goals.* There are many ways in which the components of SBM (autonomy-participation and accountability) may be combined and implemented—who gets what powers—and that makes each SBM reform unique. From the outset, therefore, it is important to be clear and precise about the goal of each SBM program. The most common

goals so far have been (1) to increase parent and community involvement in schools, (2) to empower principals and teachers, (3) to improve student achievement levels, (4) to make school management more accountable, and (5) to increase the transparency of education decision making. These different goals have significant implications for how each program is designed.

6. *Base interventions on whatever evidence is available and include a strong impact evaluation component that is appropriate for the program, its duration, and its time frame.* There are three ways to do this. First, there are evaluations that randomly select treatment schools (those that will implement an SBM project) and control schools. Second, there are evaluations in which schools' program entry order is randomized. And, third, there are evaluations that encourage schools to participate in the program. The ideal evaluation will involve some form of randomization. However, if randomizing is not an option, there are two alternative ways of estimating the reform's impact. First, an RDD procedure may be used when the program targets some continuous variable as the entry criterion. The estimation yields the true effect of the intervention without the need for randomizing in the design of the program. The second nonrandomized way to evaluate impact uses a nonrandom phase-in strategy. For this evaluation method to be technically sound, it is crucial to show that the group of schools treated later is the right counterfactual for the group of schools that initially enters the program; in other words, both groups need to have similar pretreatment observable characteristics. That requirement highlights the need for good preintervention data as well as good postintervention data to enable a comparison of the values of the outcome variables both before and after the program to measure its effects. The third method is based on the availability of a valid instrument to estimate the program by either IV or Heckman correction model. Finally, if the rule of entry into the program is completely specified by observable variables, the effect of the program can be estimated using propensity and matching estimators.

Although some positive evidence from the more rigorous evaluations of SBM programs is beginning to emerge, in the case of most SBM models in developing countries it is not yet clear how school decentralization eventually will affect student performance. The hope is that greater parental (and community) involvement will mean that school managers become more responsive to local needs and concerns and make decisions that are in the interests of the students. Another hope is that parents will become unpaid or minimally paid auxiliary staff helping teachers in classrooms and with other minor activities. Because parents are members of the local community, the further hope is that parental support for SBM will encourage local community leaders to put schools higher on their political agendas and thus provide the schools with more material resources. Furthermore, the presumed costs of reform are likely to be much smaller than the benefits, thereby increasing the appeal of the reform. Many SBM reforms have multiple goals that include participation as an outcome in itself, rather than as a means to an end such as improving learning outcomes. Other SBM reforms have encouraged parental interest in the school as a way to supplement its recurrent-cost financing. It is important to keep the goals of the program clear, to ensure that adequate resources go into the program to fulfill its specific goals, and to take capacity constraints into account. It can be very difficult to implement complex reforms with multiple goals and limited resources in a constrained environment.

Thereafter, the expectation is that the school climate—teachers' motivation, their knowledge of pedagogy, the quality of the curriculum in terms of imparting knowledge, the eagerness of students to learn, and the extent to which parents support their children's learning—will improve as the stakeholders work together in a collegial way to manage the school. However, the possibility exists that teachers and principals may come to resent being monitored constantly by parents and school council members, and that resentment may cause relationships within the school to deteriorate.

## Caveats

Decentralization or devolution does not necessarily put more power in the hands of the general public. This fact may explain the pattern in terms of the types of SBM that have been introduced in developing countries. SBM reforms of the strongest type appear to have been introduced and been successful in achieving their goals either in developed countries (such as Australia, New Zealand, and Spain), in countries coming out of conflict situations (El Salvador and Nicaragua) or natural disasters (Honduras), and in countries where the government has made SBM reforms a national priority (Qatar). Most developing countries, however, appear to be experimenting with the limited or more moderate forms of SBM—Brazil, Mexico, and some African and South Asian countries. This pattern may reflect the presence or absence of community or social structures needed to support strong SBM reforms. Those countries where democracy does not have deep roots or countries where the population is not aware of its rights are experimenting with limited forms of SBM. Countries where individuals are more aware of their rights and have some power to hold the government accountable have introduced stronger forms of SBM. In addition, there are those countries where communities have been forced by some calamity, such as war or a natural disaster, to come together as a group and find ways to deliver basic services, including education (as in the case of the Central American countries). In other words, the particular type of SBM introduced in any given country depends (or should depend) on the political economy of that particular country.

Thus, we can conclude that the conception and design of SBM programs are extremely important, perhaps more so than for any other kind of education intervention. Different types of SBM reforms may be successful under different circumstances, but no general lessons are available at this time.

## Unanswered Questions

Because of the dearth of evidence on the impact and effectiveness of SBM in practice, we still have a number of questions that must go unanswered until more evidence is available. The increasing number of evaluations going on at present—in Indonesia, Kenya, Nepal, Pakistan, and Sri Lanka, among other places—will teach us a lot about the effectiveness of SBM in various contexts. As the knowledge base grows, researchers need to pay more attention to the specific outcomes that are produced by different forms of SBM. For example, do administrative-control SBMs work better than, say, professional-control ones, and in what situations? Does more autonomy devolved to the school level improve intermediate and long-term outcomes? What sort of accountability arrangements work best and under what conditions? What role do parents play in practice? Do they need to be active participants in school management? What about the role of the larger community and its degree of participation? And is there a difference by countries' levels of development? Does it matter if the form of SBM is strong or weak? Do the number and type of functions devolved to school managers make a difference to the outcomes? Does it matter which group is given the decision-making authority and over what functions?

Also, more cost-benefit analysis is needed. SBM clearly can be a very inexpensive initiative when it constitutes only a change in the locus of decision making and not in the amount of resources in the system. If the few positive impact evaluations that exist are true, then SBM is a very cost-effective initiative. For example, the rural school-based management program in Mexico is estimated to cost about $6 per student—in unit cost terms, only about 8 percent of primary education unit expenditures.

Other elements that will need more analysis as the study of SBM reforms evolves over time are political economy issues (such as the roles played by teachers' unions and political elites) and issues of governance. SBM, like any other kind of reform, requires some level of political support from the government. In fact, political support may be more important than technical merit in the success or failure of a strong reform. Teachers and their unions may want to resist SBM reforms that give parents and community members more power. How they react to the reform is a key factor in its eventual success or failure. Even local authorities may react negatively to what they perceive as the capture of governance at various levels by elite groups, particularly if these groups use SBM reforms as means to further their political agendas. Also, there often are challenges involved in implementing SBM reform that can undermine its potential. These challenges include the need for all the relevant actors to accept and support the reform, the fact that greater time and work demands are placed on teachers and parents, and the need for more local district support.

In general, national governments can take a number of steps to increase the probability that SBM reforms will succeed. First, central governments can make local education authorities more accountable by requiring them to involve all school stakeholders in their discussions and to use the feedback that is generated to design policies and interventions that meet local needs. Meanwhile, national governments should design prospective impact evaluations of new programs before they are implemented. Furthermore, they could subject more existing programs to rigorous impact evaluations, perhaps conducted by a dedicated group within the Ministry of Education devoted to analysis and research; and at the same time encourage independent organizations to undertake their own impact evaluations of all programs. Finally, there is a need for governments—and international agencies—to spread the word about the experience of SBM innovations at the school level and to disseminate examples of best practices of SBM programs from around the world.

# Some Evaluated School-Based Management Programs

| Year of program | Country | Program description | Selection of schools/communities | Scope |
|---|---|---|---|---|
| 1982 | Brazil | Decentralization: direct transfer of funds to schools, election of principals, and creation of local school councils | Phased in | All schools |
| 1991 | El Salvador | EDUCO: community associations are responsible for administering funds, hiring and firing teachers, and monitoring and maintaining infrastructure | Municipalities and national government (with the help of promoters) identify communities | Not all schools in the country participate |
| 1991 and 1993 | Nicaragua | ASP: in 1991, established consultative councils; in 1993, transformed into management boards; wide scope of autonomous decisions | Teachers vote on the decision to enter the program | Not all schools in the country participate |
| 1996 | Mexico | AGEs: give parents' associations small amounts of money for civil works and infrastructure | National government targets areas; phase-in program: first indigenous populations, lagging primary schools, disadvantaged rural areas | Targets schools in rural areas |
| 1999 | Honduras | PROHECO: school councils have autonomy over hiring and firing teachers, monitoring and managing funds, and maintaining infrastructure | National government targets rural schools affected by Hurricane Mitch; social promoters approach communities to raise awareness and help in the process | Not all schools in the country participate |
| 2001 | Mexico | PEC: gives schools resources to implement a school plan, in consultation with parents; part of the money goes toward maintaining infrastructure and part goes toward improving teacher quality | National government targets areas; voluntary, disadvantaged urban areas | Priority given to disadvantaged rural areas |
| 2006–08 | Kenya | ETP with SBM component | Randomized selection of treatment and control schools | Small pilot group of schools |

*Sources:* Authors' compilation; di Gropello 2006; Paes de Barros and Mendonça 1998; and Gertler, Rubio-Codina, and Patrinos 2006.

*Note:* AGEs = Support to School Management program; ASP = Autonomous School Program; EDUCO = Education with Community Participation; ETP = Extra Teacher Program; PEC = Quality Schools Program; PROHECO = Community-Based Education.

# References

Abu-Duhou, Ibtisam. 1999. *School-Based Management*. Fundamentals of Educational Planning 62. Paris: UNESCO/International Institute for Educational Planning.

Akyeampong, Kwame. 2004. "Whole School Development: Ghana." Unpublished manuscript, UNESCO, Paris. http://portal.unesco.org/education/fr/ev.php-URL_ID=36145&URL_DO=DO_PRINTPAGE&URL_SECTION=201.html [accessed March 26, 2009].

Alderman, Harold. 1998. "Social Assistance in Albania: Decentralization and Targeted Transfers." Living Standards Measurement Series Working Paper 134, World Bank, Washington, DC.

Anderson, Jo Anne. 2005. *Accountability in Education*. Education Policy Series. Paris: UNESCO/International Institute for Educational Planning and International Academy of Education.

Angrist, Joshua D., and Guido W. Imbens. 1995. "Two-Stage Least Squares Estimation of Average Causal Effects in Models with Variable Treatment Intensity." *Journal of the American Statistical Association* 90 (430): 431–42.

Arcia, Gustavo, Emilio Porta Pallais, and José Ramón Laguna. 2004. "Otro vistazo a la autonomía escolar de Nicaragua: Aceptación y percepción en 2004" (Another Look at School Autonomy in Nicaragua: Agreement and Perception in 2004). General Direction of Research and Policy, Ministry of Education, Culture and Sports, Managua, Nicaragua.

Athey, Susan, and Guido W. Imbens. 2006. "Identification and Inference in Nonlinear Difference-in-Difference Models." *Econometrica* 74 (2): 431–97.

Bardhan, Pranab. 2002. "Decentralization of Governance and Development." *Journal of Economic Perspectives* 16 (4): 185–205.

Bardhan, Pranab, and Dilip Mookherjee. 2000. "Capture and Governance at the Local and National Levels." *American Economic Review* 90 (2): 135–39.

———. 2006. "Decentralization and Accountability in Infrastructure Delivery in Developing Countries." *Economic Journal* 116 (1): 101–27.

Barnett, W. Steven. 1996. "Economics of School Reform: Three Promising Models." In *Holding Schools Accountable—Performance-Based Reform in Education*, ed. Helen F. Ladd, 299–326. Washington, DC: Brookings Institution Press.

Bauer, Scott C. 1996. "Site-Based Management: A Design Perspective." Unpublished PhD diss., Cornell University, Ithaca, NY.

———. 1998. "Designing Site-Based Systems, Deriving a Theory of Practice." *International Journal of Educational Reform* 7 (2): 108–21.

Bauer, Scott C., Ira E. Bogotch, and Hae-Seong Park. 1998. "Modeling Site-Based Decision-making: The Relationship between Inputs, Site Council Practices, and Outcomes." Paper presented at the Annual Meeting of the American Educational Research Association, San Diego, CA, April 13–17.

Benveniste, Luis, and Jeffery Marshall. 2004. "School Grants and Student Performance: Evidence from the EQIP Project in Cambodia." Unpublished manuscript, World Bank, Washington, DC.

Borman, Geoffrey D., Gina M. Hewes, Laura T. Overman, and Shelly Brown. 2002. "Comprehensive School Reform and Student Achievement: A Meta-Analysis." Report No. 59, University of North Carolina, Greensboro.

———. 2003. "Comprehensive School Reform and Achievement: A Meta-Analysis." *Review of Educational Research* 73 (2): 125–230.

Brewer, Dominic J., Catherine H. Augustine, Gail L. Zellman, Gary Ryan, Charles A. Goldman, Cathleen Stasz, and Louay Constant. 2007. *Education for a New Era: Design and Implementation of K–12 Education Reform in Qatar.* Santa Monica, CA: RAND Corporation.

Briggs, Kerri, and Priscilla Wohlstetter. 1999. "Key Elements of a Successful School-Based Management Strategy." Working paper, University of Southern California, Los Angeles.

Bryk, Anthony S., Yeow Meng Thum, John Q. Easton, and Stuart Luppescu. 1998. *Academic Productivity of Chicago Public Elementary Schools: A Technical Report Sponsored by the Consortium on Chicago School Research.* Examining Productivity Series. http://ccsr.uchicago.edu/publications/p0a010.pdf [accessed March 26, 2009].

Caldwell, Brian J. 2005. *School-Based Management*. Education Policy Series. Paris: UNESCO/International Institute for Educational Planning and International Academy of Education.

Carnoy, Martin, Amber Gove, Susanna Loeb, Jeffery Marshall, and Miguel Socias. 2008. "How Schools and Students Respond to School Improvement Programs: The Case of Brazil's PDE." *Economics of Education Review* 27 (1): 22–38.

CIEN (Centro de Investigaciones Económicas Nacionales). 1999. "La Experiencia del Programa Nacional de Autogestión Para el Desarrollo Educativo PRONADE." Executive Summary, Guatemala City, Guatemala.

Cook, Thomas D. 2007. "School-Based Management in the United States." Background paper prepared for the programmatic study on school-based management, World Bank, Washington, DC.

Cook, Thomas D., H. David Hunt, and Robert F. Murphy. 2000. "Comer's School Development Program in Chicago: A Theory-Based Evaluation." *American Educational Research Journal* 37 (2): 535–97.

De Grauwe, Anton. 2005. "Improving the Quality of Education through School-Based Management: Learning from International Experiences." *International Review of Education* 51 (4): 269–87.

di Gropello, Emanuela. 2006. *A Comparative Analysis of School-Based Management in Central America*. Working Paper 72. Washington, DC: World Bank.

di Gropello, Emanuela, and Jeffery H. Marshall. 2005. "Teacher Effort and Schooling Outcomes in Rural Honduras." In *Incentives to Improve Teaching: Lessons from Latin America*, ed. Emiliana Vegas, 307–58. Washington, DC: World Bank.

Dimmock, Clive, and Allan Walker. 1998a. "Comparative Educational Administration: Developing a Cross-Cultural Conceptual Framework." *Educational Administration Quarterly* 34 (4): 558–95.

———. 1998b. "Transforming Hong Kong's Schools: Trends and Emerging Issues." *Journal of Educational Administration* 36 (5): 476–91.

Drury, Darrel, and Douglas Levin. 1994. "School-Based Management: The Changing Locus of Control in American Public Education." Prepared by Pelavin Associates for the Office of Educational Research, U.S. Department of Education, Washington, DC.

Duflo, Esther, Pascaline Dupas, and Michael Kremer. 2007. "Peer Effects, Pupil-Teacher Ratios, and Teacher Incentives: Evidence from a Randomization Evaluation in Kenya." Unpublished manuscript, Poverty Action Lab, Massachusetts Institute of Technology, Cambridge, MA.

Duflo, Esther, Rachel Glennerster, and Michael Kremer. 2006. "Using Randomization in Development Economics Research: A Toolkit." Technical Working Paper 333, National Bureau of Economic Research, Cambridge, MA.

Duflo, Esther, and Emmanuel Saez. 2003. "The Role of Information and Social Interactions in Retirement Plan Decisions: Evidence from a Randomized Experiment." *Quarterly Journal of Economics* 118 (3): 815–42.

Edge, Karen. 2000. "El Salvador: EDUCO." In *Decentralization and School-Based Management Resource Kit-Case Studies*. Washington, DC: World Bank.

Faguet, Jean-Paul. 2001. "Does Decentralization Increase Government Responsiveness to Local Needs? Decentralization and Public Investment in Bolivia." Working paper, Center for Economic Performance, London School of Economics.

Fisman, Raymond, and Roberta Gatti. 2002. "Decentralization and Corruption: Evidence across Countries." *Journal of Public Economics* 83: 325–45.

Gaziel, Haim. 1998. "School-Based Management as a Factor in School Effectiveness." *International Review of Education* 44 (4): 319–33.

Geeves, Richard, Chin Vanny, Kuoy Pharin, Ly Sereyrith, Song Heng, and Tran Pancharun. 2002. *Evaluation of the Impact of the Education Quality Improvement Project (EQIP) of the Ministry of Education, Youth and Sport of the Royal Government of Cambodia*. Phnom Penh, Cambodia: World Education Cambodia.

Gertler, Paul, Harry A. Patrinos, and Marta Rubio-Codina. 2007. "Methodological Issues in the Evaluation of School-Based Management Reforms." Unpublished manuscript, World Bank, Washington, DC.

Gertler, Paul J., Marta Rubio-Codina, and Harry A. Patrinos. 2006. "Empowering Parents to Improve Education. Evidence from Rural Mexico." Policy Research Working Paper 3935, World Bank, Washington, DC.

Gunnarsson, Victoria, Peter F. Orazem, Mario Sanchez, and Aimee Verdisco. 2004. "Does School Decentralization Raise Student Outcomes? Theory and Evidence on the Roles of School Autonomy and Community Participation." Unpublished manuscript, Iowa State University, Ames.

Hanushek, Eric A., and Ludger Woessmann. 2007. "The Role of Education Quality in Economic Growth." Policy Research Working Paper 4122, World Bank, Washington, DC.

Heckman, James J. 1976. "The Common Structure of Statistical Models of Truncation, Sample Selection, and Limited Dependent Variables and a Simple Estimator for Such Models." *Annals of Economic and Social Measurement* 5 (4): 475–92.

Heckman, James J., Hidehiko Ichimura, and Petra Todd. 1998. "Matching as an Econometric Evaluation Estimator." *Review of Economic Studies* 65 (2): 261–94.

Hess, G. Alfred Jr., ed. 1996. *Implementing Reform: Stories of Stability and Change in 14 Schools*. Chicago, IL: Chicago Panel on School Policy.

———. 1999. "Expectations, Opportunity, Capacity and Will: The Four Essential Components of Chicago School Reform." *Educational Policy* 13 (4): 494–517.

Hirano Keisuke, Guido W. Imbens, Donald B. Rubin, and Xiao-Hua Zhou. 2000. "Assessing the Effect of an Influenza Vaccine in an Encouragement Design." *Biostatistics* 1: 69–88.

Jimenez, Emmanuel, and Yasuyuki Sawada. 1999. "Do Community-Managed Schools Work? An Evaluation of El Salvador's EDUCO Program." *World Bank Economic Review* 13 (3): 415–41.

———. 2003. "Does Community Management Help Keep Kids in Schools? Evidence Using Panel Data from El Salvador's EDUCO Program." Discussion Paper, Center for International Research on the Japanese Economy, University of Tokyo.

Karim, Shahnaz, Claudia A. Santizo Rodall, and Enrique Cabrero Mendoza. 2004. *Transparency in Education.* Paris: UNESCO/International Institute for Educational Planning and International Academy of Education.

King, Elizabeth M., and Susana Cordeiro-Guerra. 2005. "Education Reforms in East Asia: Policy, Process, and Impact." In *East Asia Decentralizes: Making Local Government Work*, 179–208. Washington, DC: World Bank.

King, Elizabeth M., Peter F. Orazem, and Victoria Gunnarsson. 2003. "Decentralization and Student Achievement: International Evidence on the Roles of School Autonomy and Community Participation." Paper presented at the Fourth Annual Global Development Conference on Globalization and Equity, Cairo, Egypt, January 19–21.

King, Elizabeth M., and Berk Özler. 1998. "What's Decentralization Got to Do with Learning? The Case of Nicaragua's School Autonomy Reform." Unpublished manuscript, Development Research Group, World Bank, Washington, DC.

King, Elizabeth M., Berk Özler, and Laura B. Rawlings. 1999. "Nicaragua's School Autonomy Reform: Fact or Fiction?" Working Paper Series on Impact Evaluation of Education Reforms, Paper No. 19, Development Research Group, World Bank, Washington, DC.

Lee, Valerie E., Julia B. Smith, Tamara E. Perry, and Mark A. Smylie. 1999. "Social Support, Academic Press, and Student Achievement. A View from the Middle Grades in Chicago." University of Michigan, Ann Arbor. http://ccsr.uchicago.edu/publications/p0e01.pdf [accessed March 26, 2009].

Leithwood, Kenneth, and Teresa Menzies. 1998. "Forms and Effects of School-Based Management: A Review." *Educational Policy* 12 (3): 325–46.

Lopez-Calva, Luis Felipe, and Luis D. Espinosa. 2006. "Efectos diferenciales de los programas compensatorios del CONAFE en el aprovechamiento escolar." In *Efectos del Impulso a la Participación de los Padres de Familia en la Escuela* (Effects of Parental Participation in the School), ed. Antonio Blanco Lerín. Mexico City: Consejo Nacional de Fomento Educativo.

Malen, Barry, Rodney T. Ogawa, and Jennifer Kranz. 1990. "What Do We Know about Site-Based Management: A Case Study of the Literature—A Call for Research." In *Choice and Control in American Education: The Practice of Choice, Decentralization and School Restructuring, Volume 2*, ed. William H. Clune and John F. White, 289–342. London: Falmer Press.

Marshall, Jeffery H. 2004. "If You Build It, Will They Come? Primary School Quality and Grade Attainment in Rural Guatemala." PhD diss., School of Education, Stanford University, Palo Alto, CA.

MINEDUC (Guatemala, Ministry of Education). 2004. "Anuario Estadístico 2002" (Annual Satistics 2002). Guatemala City.

MINEDUC/DP Tecnología. 2002. "Estudio Quasi-Experimental de Resultados de PRONADE 2001" (Quasi-experimental Study of Results of PRONADE 2001). Guatemala City.

Montreal Economic Institute. 2007. "Decentralization of School Management: Ideas from Abroad." *Economic Note* (Education Series), February. http://www.iedm.org/uploaded/pdf/fevrier07b_en.pdf [accessed March 27, 2009].

Murnane, Richard J., John B. Willet, and Sergio Cardenas. 2006. "Did the Participation of Schools in *Programa Escuelas de Calidad* (PEC) Influence Student Outcomes?" Working paper, Graduate School of Education, Harvard University, Cambridge, MA.

Nir, Adam E. 2002. "School-Based Management and Its Effect on Teacher Commitment." *International Journal of Leadership in Education* 5 (4): 323–41.

OECD (Organisation for Economic Co-operation and Development). 2004. "Policy Brief: Raising the Quality of Educational Performance at School." Organisation for Economic Co-operation and Development, Paris. http://www.oecd.org/dataoecd/17/8/29472036.pdf [accessed March 27, 2009].

Paes de Barros, Roberto, and Rosane Mendonça. 1998. "The Impact of Three Institutional Innovations in Brazilian Education." In *Organization Matters: Agency Problems in Health and Education in Latin America*, ed. William D. Savedoff, 75–130. Washington, DC: Inter-American Development Bank.

Parker, Caroline E. 2005. "Teacher Incentives and Student Achievement in Nicaraguan Autonomous Schools." In *Incentives to Improve Teaching: Lessons from Latin America*, ed. Emiliana Vegas, 359–88. Washington, DC: World Bank.

Patrinos, Harry A., and Ruth Kagia. 2007. "Maximizing the Performance of Education Systems: The Case of Teacher Absenteeism." In *The Many Faces of Corruption—Tracking Vulnerabilities at the Sector Level*, J. Edgardo Campos and Sanjay Pradhan, 63–88. Washington, DC: World Bank.

Reinikka, Ritva, and Jakob Svensson. 2004. "Explaining Leakage of Public Funds." Policy Research Working Paper 2709, World Bank, Washington, DC.

Rosenbaum, Paul R., and Donald B. Rubin. 1983. "The Central Role of the Propensity Score in Observational Studies for Causal Effects." *Biometrika* 70 (1): 41–55.

Rowan, Brian, Eric Camburn, and Carol Barnes. 2004. "Benefiting from Comprehensive School Reform: A Review of Research on CSR Implementation." In *Putting Pieces Together: Lessons from Comprehensive School Reform Research*, ed. Christopher T. Cross, 1–52. Washington, DC: National Clearinghouse for Comprehensive School Reform.

Santibañez, Lucrecia. 2006. "School-Based Management Effects on Educational Outcomes: A Literature Review and Assessment of the Evidence Base." Working paper, World Bank, Washington, DC.

Sawada, Yasuyuki. 2000. "Community Participation, Teacher Effort, and Educational Outcome: The Case of El Salvador's EDUCO Program." Working Paper 307, William Davidson Institute, University of Michigan, Ann Arbor.

Sawada, Yasuyuki, and Andrew B. Ragatz. 2005. "Decentralization of Education, Teacher Behavior and Outcomes: The Case of El Salvador's EDUCO Program." In *Incentives to Improve Teaching: Lessons from Latin America*, ed. Emiliana Vegas, 255–306. Washington, DC: World Bank.

Shadish, William, Thomas D. Cook, and Donald T. Campbell. 2002. *Experimental and Quasi-Experimental Designs for Generalized Causal Inference*. Boston: Houghton Mifflin.

Shapiro, Joseph S., and Emmanuel Skoufias. 2006. "Local but Unequal? How Educational Decentralization Stratifies Schools." Unpublished manuscript, World Bank, Washington, DC.

Shipps, Dorothy, Joseph Kahne, and Mark A. Smylie. 1999. "The Politics of Urban School Reform: Legitimacy, City Growth, and School Improvement in Chicago." *Educational Policy* 13 (4): 518–45.

Skoufias, Emmanuel, and Joseph Shapiro. 2006. "Evaluating the Impact of Mexico's Quality Schools Program: The Pitfalls of Using Nonexperimental Data." Impact Evaluation Series 8, Policy Research Working Paper 4036, World Bank, Washington, DC.

Transparency International. 2005. *Stealing the Future: Corruption in the Classroom*. Berlin, Germany: Transparency International. http://www.transparency. org/publications/publications/stealing_future [accessed March 24, 2009].

Wantchékon, Leonard. 2008. "School-Based Management, Media Access and Education Outcomes in Benin: Experimental Evidence from Benin." Unpublished manuscript, New York University, New York.

Wohlstetter, Priscilla, and Susan A. Mohrman. 1996. *Assessment of School-based Management. Volume I: Findings and Conclusions*. Los Angeles: University of Southern California.

Wong, Evia O.W. 2003. "Leadership Style for School-Based Management in Hong Kong." *International Journal of Educational Management* 17 (6): 243–47.

World Bank. 2003. *World Development Report 2004: Making Services Work for Poor People.* Washington, DC: World Bank.

———. 2004. "Guatemala—Equity and Student Achievement in Primary Education." Volumes I and II, Report No. 22691, World Bank, Washington, DC.

———. 2008a. "BOS and BOS-KITA Project Appraisal Document." Indonesia Report No, 45043-ID, World Bank, Washington, DC.

———. 2008b. "Devolving Power to the Local Level: The Role of Information and Capacity Building in Empowering Community-Based Organizations." Concept Note on Ghana, World Bank, Washington, DC.

———. 2008c. "Mozambique DSSP: Case Study for the Africa SBM Report." Unpublished manuscript, World Bank, Washington, DC.

———. 2008d. "Rwanda Impact Evaluation Incentives and Performance for Teachers on Fixed Contracts." Concept Note, World Bank, Washington, DC.

———. 2008e. "Senegal: Evaluation of the Impact of School Grants on Education Achievement." Concept Note, World Bank, Washington, DC.

Wylie, Cathy. 1996. "Finessing Site-Based Management with Balancing Acts." *Educational Leadership* 53 (4): 54–57.

# Index

*Boxes, figures, notes, and tables are indicated by b, f, n, and t, respectively.*